AF521824

DEDICATION

The concept of this book came from my personal admiration for Mario Andretti and Dan Gurney, as well as from the passion demonstrated by the entire Circuit of The Americas team. Their dedication, persistence and commitment delivered what we think is the best new track in the Formula 1 World Championship. An amazing challenge that I personally had the privilege to follow closely nearly every day, while also discovering the United States' incredible heritage in Grand Prix racing. This book is dedicated to all the American drivers, teams, manufacturers, sponsors, and to the Circuit of The Americas team, who made it happen. This year's event represents a new chapter in the history of Formula 1 as the Texas Grand Prix opens up a new frontier for future American drivers.

We are grateful to Mario Andretti for writing the foreword to this book. Special thanks goes to Geoff Moore, Julie Loignon and Regan Holley from the Circuit of The America's PR and Marketing teams.

Jean Paul Libert
Chief Publishing Officer

THE AMERICAN LEGACY IN FORMULA 1

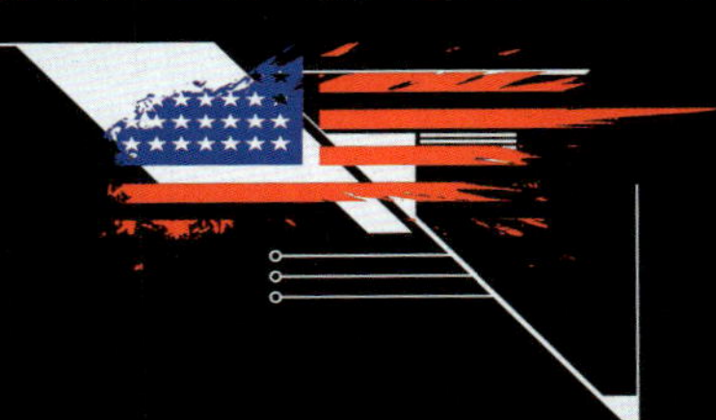

Phillip van Osten

Bernard & Paul-Henri Cahier

Publisher
The Dojupa Group, LLC.
5586 Kirkwood Highway
Wilmington, DE 19808

Chief Executive Officer
Jean Paul Libert

Marketing and Creative
Velocity, Inc.
1020 James Dr., #101
Leesport, PA 19533

Creative Director
Robert W. Hudepohl, Jr.
Art Director and Designer
Chris L. Parr

Author
Phillip van Osten
Editorial Contributors
Pierre Van Vliet
Alain van den Abeele
COTA Coordinator
Julie Koenig Loignon

Photography
The Cahier Archive
www.f1-photo.com

Additional Photos
World Racing Images
www.wri2.net

Photographic Selection
Pierre Van Vliet
Studio Production
Emeric de Baré
Coordinator
Kathleen Bimson

ISBN 978 0 9884290 0 0

Price $ 99,95

CONTENTS

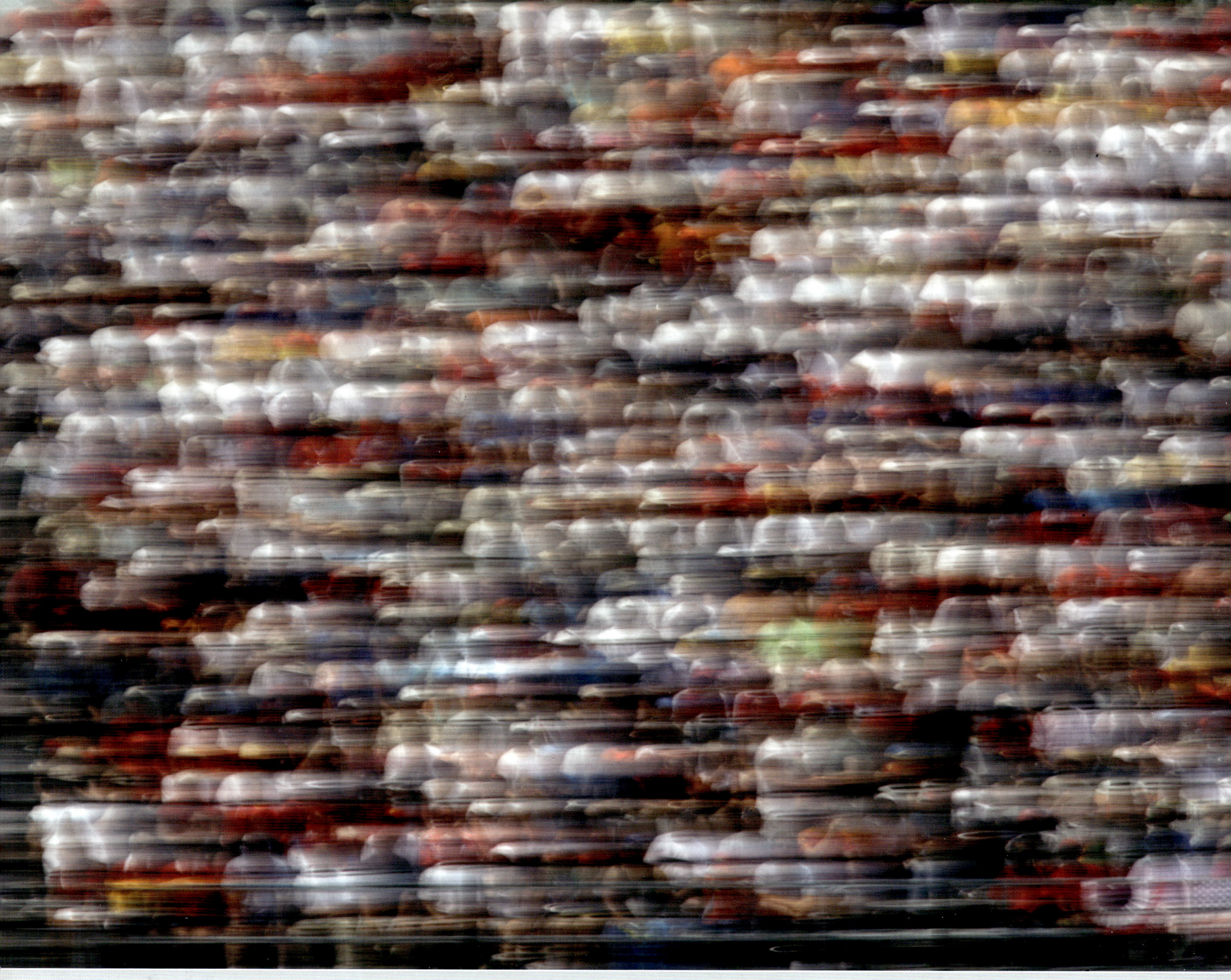

A WORD FROM BOBBY & RED

The pages within this book contain the story of America's history with Formula One™ racing and the birth of F1's newest U.S. home in Austin, Texas. The story of how Circuit of The Americas came to be – and its quest to become the world's greatest place to experience racing and entertainment – is a fascinating tale unto itself. Whether you're a competitor or patron, you'll be amazed by this facility and what it was designed to do both as a place to experience great spectacles and as a local business created to be a significant economic engine for its home region.

Circuit of the Americas is more than just a racetrack, although its 3.4-mile undulating circuit is certainly a distinctive feature. The 350-acre venue also features the largest amphitheater in Central Texas, an iconic 250-foot tower offering breath-taking views of the countryside, more than 300,000-square feet of premium hospitality space and lots of room for future development. The Circuit and its world-class facilities are intended to draw more than one million visitors annually to Central Texas, while creating meaningful jobs and community partnerships. Most important, Circuit of The Americas will be a place where family and friends come to enjoy fun and fellowship together.

Though our company is young, as an economic engine, we're revved up and accelerating. Nearly 5,000 families have received direct income from jobs related to the construction of the $300-million dollar facility made possible through private investment. The first "race" won at the Circuit was the competition to complete the facility in record time, and we owe a tremendous debt to the men and women who worked long hours to make our vision a reality.

I know Circuit of The Americas will create new jobs and opportunities for the State of Texas, and I also hope it creates new memories for fans around the world that come to Austin to experience premier racing and entertainment. Nothing would give me greater pleasure than to see parents and children make a visit to Circuit of The Americas part of their unique, family tradition…that would be a true victory!

As you immerse yourself in The American Legacy in Formula One, I invite you to enjoy America's remarkable past in this one-of-a-kind sport, while also looking forward to Formula 1's bright future at its new American home at Circuit of The Americas.

Warm regards,

Bobby Epstein
Chairman and Founding Partner
Circuit of The Americas

When I was approached about offering financial and management involvement of what is now the Circuit of The Americas, I had very little knowledge of Formula 1™ racing. Seeing the impact that this sport had worldwide with no successful American operation was a challenge.

With the assistance of my loving and active family, and Rad Weaver and Bruce Knox from my corporate staff, I joined with Bobby Epstein to create the finest motorsport facility in the world, featuring Formula 1 racing with other major sports activities year round.

The challenges have been great but I am very excited that we will offer year-round activities with world-class stature. I did not do this for myself. I did this for the great sports fans that make this possible.

I anticipate experiencing the rewards of genuine excitement and sheer joy during the many events of our inaugural season, and I invite you to participate with us in this thrilling opportunity.

Sincerely,

Red McCombs
Founding Partner
Circuit of The Americas

2012 FORMULA 1
UNITED STATES GRAND PRIX
ADMIT ONE: BERNIE ECCLESTONE
MAIN GRANDSTAND
SECTION: VIP
ROW: A
NOVEMBER 16·17·18 AUSTIN, TEXAS
2012 FORMULA 1
UNITED STATES
GRAND PRIX

DEAR RACING ENTHUSIAST

The world's most popular motorsport, Formula One™ racing, boasts a long and proud tradition here in the United States – and a rather uneven storyline. While the sport in the US dates back to the early 1900s and several American cities have played host to a United States Grand Prix, F1™ does not enjoy the same firm roots in this country as it does in Western Europe, which is home to Grand Prix racing's most legendary circuits. I remember falling in love with F1 as a teenager. My twin brother, Aldo, and I watched the Italian Grand Prix at the iconic Monza circuit. I'll never forget the speed and the sound of the cars and how accomplished and glamorous the drivers seemed. From that moment on, I knew I wanted to race cars professionally and experience the same exhilaration I witnessed as a fan.

I've been blessed with much success in my career, including a Formula One World Championship, and my love for racing is now part of my entire family's DNA. You could say racing is a way of life for the Andrettis. This commemorative book, The American Legacy in Formula 1, shares the stories of several American racing drivers who, like me, had the incredible opportunity to compete with the best of the best in Formula One.

While their stories are part of F1's past, the sport is embracing an invigorated future here in the United States, this time with a new state-of-the-art home at Circuit of The Americas™ in Austin, Texas. This impressive 1300-acre development is more than just a purpose-built Grand Prix facility featuring the country's only Grade 1 race course. Circuit of The Americas is a premier destination for a wide variety of sporting, business, entertainment and leisure events and will be a tremendous economic driver for its home state and surrounding region.

As Circuit of The Americas' official ambassador, I am honored to welcome you back into F1's ever-evolving story in the United States and to share with you the remarkable tale of how its new Texas home came to be. I hope to see you at Circuit of The Americas for the FORMULA 1 UNITED STATES GRAND PRIX™.

INTRODUCTION

Looking back on our country's first formative century, and well beyond, America's extraordinary development was all about the drive of 'heading West'. From the early European emigrants who settled on the Eastern seaboard, to their descendants who extended the trend of westward expansion to the Appalachian Mountains, and then to the Pacific, western movement was a landmark phenomenon in American history. As the fabric of the United States was woven by settlers' dreams of a better life, unprecedented prosperity and progress emerged, fuelling further waves of migration to the Promised Land.

From the world's industrial revolution, the automobile was born, and with it unfolded a whole new frontier of mobility and speed. Motor racing started in France with the great city to city races, like the Paris to Rouen event held in 1894. In 1899, James Gordon Bennett, the Paris-based millionaire owner of the *New York Herald*, offered a trophy to be raced for annually on the sandy and rough European roads by the automobile clubs of various countries. In 1904, an international event was also founded in the United States by Williams Kassam Vanderbilt II. The first Vanderbilt Cup consisted of a race run over a 30-mile course of winding dirt roads through Nassau County on Long Island, New York. Its large cash prize encouraged the top drivers and their machines from across the Atlantic to head west in a successful quest to defeat their American counterparts. In 1906, the Automobile Club de France organized a race on a proper closed circuit – or rather itinerary – located on the outskirts of the city of Le Mans. It was the first event to carry the name 'Grand Prix'. American representation in the milestone race was limited to a few expatriates driving French manufactured cars, but in 1908 the United States staged its own 'Grand Prize' with an event held in Savannah, Georgia. On the 25-mile course, European drivers and their advanced machines succeeded once again in upstaging the US opposition, but only after local hero Ralph DePalma – an Italian immigrant driving for Lancia – was side-lined with mechanical trouble after becoming the first American to lead a Grand Prix.

In the early part of the century, France had established itself as the cradle of motor racing, while Europe clearly held the upper hand in automobile design and craftsmanship. Well aware of this dominance, an Indiana businessman named Carl Fisher, along with several partners, decided to build a dedicated race track set just outside the city of Indianapolis, where so many horseless carriage manufacturers were located. The 2.5-mile oval circuit opened in the summer of 1909, with an estimated 80,000 people in attendance at the first 500-mile race on Memorial Day, May 30, 1911. Ray Harroun's triumph at the wheel of his Marmon Wasp set in motion a golden age for motor racing in the United States and for the celebrated Speedway.

At the time, American drivers competing abroad were scarce while American cars racing in Europe were even more uncommon. Foreign presence in the United States on the other hand was abundant, and thriving, with Peugeot and Mercedes claiming a string of wins at the Brickyard from 1913 to 1916. Slowly but surely the Americans caught on however, taking ownership of the Indianapolis 500 from 1919, when racing resumed after the Great War, while also venturing across the Atlantic to challenge the Old World's aces and their dominant machines.

In 1921, the Automobile Club de France revived its Grand Prix event for the first time in seven years, choosing once again Le Mans as the venue, although the course's layout was different than the one used 15 years earlier. The 10.75-mile race adopted the same rules being used at Indianapolis, but the French imposed a huge entry fee in an attempt to dissuade American teams and manufacturers from participating. The plot failed miserably as not only was there a healthy American contingent, but Californian Jimmy Murphy and his famous white Duesenberg dealt a heavy blow to French pride by winning the gruelling 4-hour event. He was the first American to win a European Grand Prix, and would remain the only driver from the United States to accomplish such a feat until Phil Hill's triumph in the 1960 Italian Grand Prix. In the 1930s, the emergence of a regular calendar of events led to the growth of motor racing throughout Europe. It was also the birth of professional racing which saw the rise of factory teams such as the powerful German state-supported Mercedes and Auto Union squads. As Grand Prix racing remained firmly entrenched in its European roots, American involvement continued to be sparse up until the onset of World War II which justifiably halted all competition.

.EFT: American Jimmy Murphy powers his Duesenberg ıt Rouen in 1921. RIGHT: A scene from the first /anderbilt Cup held in 1904 in Nassau County on Long Island.

Jpon the termination of hostilities in Europe, America ekindled its focus on economic growth and prosperity, supported by a fresh flurry of immigration. The nation's automobile manufacturers relinquished their role as defense contractors to resume mass production of designs destined to become glittering symbols of the American dream. A budding interest in speed and racing captured the youth, and their enthusiasm was further invigorated in the early 1950s when imported machines from Ferrari, Maserati, Porsche, MG and Austin Healey took to the country's tracks and road courses. For the American racing driver, a change of direction was in the cards. Europe was where motor racing's heritage laid. The old continent was an aspiring champion's ultimate frontier, a fertile land of success brimming with prestigious events and coveted trophies. The time had come for the bold and audacious to travel east.

Those who left the US in search of employment with foreign teams and manufacturers incarnated a lively and attractive motor racing fresco. Their adventurous spirit led the way for future World Champions, legendary triumphs, the titanic battles between Ford and Ferrari and the unprecedented technical evolution of Formula 1.

As we look back at the various fortunes and outstanding accomplishments of these men, and the teams and manufacturers they represented, one must greatly value their contribution to motor racing history. As talented hardworking individuals, they lived their life to the fullest, but above all they were truly happy in what they did. They were the stepping stones which lined American motor racing's path from the US to international success.

DEAR RACE FANS,

Pirelli is honored to be associated with the Circuit of The Americas and the return of Formula 1 to the United States.

This revival reconnects motorsport in America with the rest of the world. U.S. drivers, fans and the industry will benefit from becoming a part of what is truly a global game of excellence, participating in a rising spiral of technology and innovation and a global viewer base unrivalled in any other sport contested on a yearly basis.

Pirelli's experience as exclusive supplier to Formula 1 has been an exciting ride thus far. Our R&D team embarked on the adventure in 2010 with a daunting task: to design, test and manufacture the tires Pirelli would supply all teams from the 2011 season onwards in just eight months. We stood up to the challenge and provided what we were asked to deliver: tires that would perform at maximum capability in varying conditions, requiring drivers to manage their pit stops strategically. This has brought two very closely contested seasons never before seen in Formula 1, with tire strategy often making the difference for a place on the podium.

For Pirelli, making the R&D investment required for Formula 1 has far-reaching benefits: the series helps connect us to our customers and consumers that elect to sell and use premium products derived from technology and experience developed at the highest level.

Circuit of The Americas will provide an exceptional stage for the world to watch as the pinnacle of racing takes center stage in the USA and it is our pleasure to help contribute to the spectacle. We look forward to opening an exciting new chapter in Formula 1 history in the United States, both for the fans who will attend in person and for the billions of viewers all over the world. May the race begin!

Paolo Ferrari

Chairman & CEO Pirelli NAFTA Region

WORLD CHAMPIONS

PHIL HILL: 1961 | MARIO ANDRETTI: 1978

BLAZING THE TRAIL

Date of birth	World Champion	First Grand Prix	Wins	Grand Prix Starts	Pole Positions
April 20, 1927	1961	France 1958	3	47	7

PHIL HILL

WORLD CHAMPION 1961

Ie put everything on the line to become America's first Formula 1 World Champion, surviving some hard-fought battles along the way. On his journey to success, Phil Hill defeated his rivals, but also his own insecurities.

'here's an old belief in motor racing that nice guys lon't win world championships. This may resonate as true in today's fiercely competitive and merciless vorld of sport, but half a century ago, well before he emergence of professionalism and big business n Formula 1, respect, solidarity and a sense of raternity were relevant to a great champion's success. Phil Hill cherished and upheld those values throughout his entire career and life. As a deeply sensitive man, he was often at odds with the perils of his profession and the inner turmoil they induced. Yet racing was the leading means by which he best accomplished himself. He was America's first Formula 1 World Champion, and as one of the greatest long-distance drivers of all time, he was also the first American-born winner at Le Mans.

Philip Toll Hill was born on April 20, 1927 in Miami, but was raised in Santa Monica, California, where his father was a postmaster. Hill was smitten by speed, power and cars early on. In fact he was barely 12 years old when he took his first car, a Model T Ford his aunt had bought him, to a dirt track in Santa Monica Canyon and went round and round. He followed his parents' wise recommendation and enrolled at the University of Southern California to study business administration for several years while also working as a mechanic on a pair of Offenshauser midgets at a time when the postwar craze for the little open-wheel machines was in full swing. The energy he devoted to his racing fervor – and the lousy grades which ensued – left Hill with little choice but to quit school. Finding a job as a mechanic at International Motors in Los Angeles, Phil acquired a supercharged MG TC in which he made his proper racing debut, winning a speedway event and getting

RIGHT ABOVE: A young and jubilant Hill celebrates victory in 1953. RIGHT: Hill's Ferrari Dino 246 roaring through the streets of Porto in the 1960 Portuguese Grand Prix.

Podiums	Fastest Laps	Points	Average Points/Race	Average Points/Season	Laps Led
16	10	98	2,09	14,00	172

LEFT: Mischievous British journalist Denis Jenkinson looks on as Phil Hill waits in the Monza pits in 1958. BOTTOM: Hill on his way to his first podium finish at Monza in 1958. RIGHT: Hill's Ferrari 156 'Sharknose' leads team mate Ginther around Casino Square in Monaco in 1961.

paid for it! After a brief spell as a trainee in Coventry, England, with the Jaguar company he returned to California with an XK 120 in which he won his first road races at Santa Ana and Pebble Beach on the Monterey Peninsula. From then on, there was no looking back for Phil Hill.

His talent and skill caught the eye of wealthy Ferrari owner Allen Guiberson who entered his 'protégé' in the 1952 Carrera Panamericana, an open road race through Mexico in which he finished sixth. The following year, he and his riding mechanic and friend Richie Ginther were fortunate to survive a huge accident after their Ferrari 350 Mexico Vignale skidded off a cliff, bounced and rolled end over end! Bot men emerged unscathed. But racing's danger started to produce their fair share of anxieties for Hi who developed severe tension, and a stomach ulce On doctor's orders, a short hiatus from racin followed in 1954 during which time he restored hi aunt's beautiful old 1931 Perce-Arrow town cabriole to mint condition. Back behind the wheel, he agai joined forces with benefactor Guiberson for sports car outings in Buenos Aires and Sebring. Hill the returned to Mexico for the Panamericana, once agai with the intrepid Ginther at his side. The pair finishe a brilliant second, winning three of the nine legs, ho on the heels of the more powerful machine o

Umberto Maglioli, Ferrari's factory driver. Hill's masterful job in the grueling road race encouraged Luigi Chinetti, Ferrari's importer for the US and owner of the North American Racing Team, to offer him several drives in his own cars. More importantly, Chinetti advised Enzo Ferrari to recruit the Californian to drive for his works team at Le Mans in 1955. Over the following five seasons, Phil Hill enjoyed an outstanding run of success with the Italian squad in sportscar racing, winning Le Mans in 1958, 1961 and 1962, sharing victory on all occasions with Belgian Olivier Gendebien. Back home, Hill won the Sebring 12-hour race in 1958, 1959 and 1961.

During his early days as a fully-fledged works Ferrari driver, Hill was aching to take the final step and drive a Grand Prix car; the ultimate racing machine. Tired of waiting for his employer's offer, he accepted to drive a private Maserati in the 1958 French Grand Prix. The race only produced a seventh place finis but Ferrari took notice and hastily contracted th American to its Grand Prix squad. Hill drove in tw championship races for the Scuderia in 1958, yet i both contributed to the title won by his teammate an idol, Mike Hawthorn. At Monza, in his first officia appearance in the Ferrari Formula 1 team, Hi qualified seventh but was leading the pack - and very surprised Stirling Moss - by several cars length at the end of the opening lap. As the race develope and pit stops organized the hierarchy, Hill wa ordered to slow by the Scuderia's team manager s that he would not take valuable championship point from Hawthorn. The American driver's very specia relationship with Ferrari and Monza was established Hill scored the first of his three Formula 1 victorie at the 1960 Italian Grand Prix, driving the now out-dated front-engine Dino 246 in a race boycotte by the British teams over the continued use o Monza's bumpy and dangerous banking. Ferrari ha extensively tested new engines for the 1.5-lite formula which came into effect in 1961, providing its trio of factory drivers (which included Hill, Wolfgang von Trips and fellow Californian Richie Ginther)

ABOVE LEFT: Hill, Cliff Allison and Dan Gurney in Argentina in 1960
ABOVE RIGHT: Hill at full speed on Monza's notorious banking on his way to his first Grand Prix win.

ABOVE: Hill and von Trips offer a subdued smile to Bernard Cahier's camera at the 1960 Targa Florio. Tragically, the German ace would lose his life at the title-deciding 1961 Italian Grand Prix. In the shot above, Ferrari engineer Carlo Chiti congratulates America's first World Champion. Needless to say, the sensitive Hill had mixed emotions about the dramatic turn of events. LEFT: Hill leading Ginther, Rodriguez and von Trips as the Ferrari squad runs together on Monza's banking.

with a powerful contender in the shape of the 156 rear-engine 'Sharknose' design. The striking machine and its drivers simply outclassed the opposition although the Lotus cars of Stirling Moss and a young Jimmy Clark mounted a fierce challenge on occasion. In the end, the race for the world title came down to just two drivers, Hill and von Trips, and one race: the Italian Grand Prix. Phil Hill's son, Derek, a former racer in his own right, recounts his father's memories of the atmosphere which proceeded the triumphant but tragic Monza weekend: "It was tremendously stressful as my father and von Trips were at the absolute edge, completely worried sick. Neither America nor Germany had ever had a world champion before." On race day, Phil Hill led the way at the start, but disaster struck on the second lap when von Trips fatally collided with Clark's Lotus. The two cars touched wheels; the Ferrari careered towards an embankment and plunged into the crowd before tumbling back onto the track in a fury of disintegrating metal. von Trips and 14 unfortunate spectators perished. Hill recalled the aftermath of the tragedy: "When they told me the news that Trips was dead, and more than a dozen spectators with him, I was stunned, deeply shocked. The papers reported that I broke down and sobbed, but that was not true. When you've lived as close to death and danger as long as I have, then your emotional defenses are equal to almost anything."

Phil Hill became a grief-stricken World Champion in 1961 but America's first champion. Nevertheless, Ferrari's dominance in Formula 1 vanished the following year and so probably did Hill's

PREVIOUS PAGE: Hill's Ferrari 156 runs through the Nürburgring's famous Karussel. LEFT: Spa offers its majestic Ardennes forest as a fitting backdrop to Hill and Rodriguez as they race up the hill to Les Combes in 1962.

motivation as a Grand Prix driver. Uncompetitive spells with the disastrous ATS and Cooper teams in 1963 and 1964 respectively, drew the curtain on this sensitive man's eminent career. He remained involved in racing as a pioneer of the Ford GT40 program as well as an active member of Jim Hall's Chaparral sportscar team. Phil Hill's last race offered a fitting conclusion to his outstanding vocation when he won the BOAC Six Hours of Brands Hatch in 1967 with Mike Spence at the wheel of the magnificent winged Chaparral 2F.

Devoting his time and energy to his passion for classic car restoration, setting up shop in Santa Monica under the Hill & Vaughn banner, Phil lived a life of contentment with his wife Alma and their two children, Vanessa and Derek, until his passing in 2008. Phil Hill's unceasing passion for all manner of automobiles inspired the famous Pebble Beach Concours d'Elegance to establish the Phil Hill Scholarships in 2009 to help fund the education of students who share his interests. 'Tonight Show' host and classic car collector extraordinaire, Jay Leno, who often sought restoration advice from Hill, offered his own befitting portrayal of the great American champion: "He was one hero who didn't disappoint you when you met him. Phil was just a modest, decent, good man, just a damn good man. He was a Packard mechanic who just happened to be a World Champion."

LEFT: Hill and Chiti confer during practice at Zandvoort in 1961. In 1963, the pair worked together as part of the breakaway ATS team, Chiti's ill-fated attempt to set up his own F1 effort. RIGHT: Hill and Ginther power through Monza's park in 1961

JAY LENO: "PHIL WAS ONE HERO WHO DIDN'T DISAPPOINT YOU WHEN YOU MET HIM."

A HEART AND SOUL ANCHORED IN RACING

Date of birth	World Champion	First Grand Prix	Wins	Grand Prix Starts	Pole Positions
February 28, 1940	1978	USA 1968	12	128	18

MARIO ANDRETTI

WORLD CHAMPION 1978

It would probably be easier to sum up the Old Testament on the back of a postcard than to write a one page summary of Mario Andretti's extraordinary achievements in motor racing. On the other hand, assessing this living legend's legacy is easy.

As the greatest all-around driver in the history of the sport, Mario Andretti won in midgets, sprint cars, stock cars, sports cars, Indy cars and Grand Prix machines. He triumphed on dirt tracks, speedways, clockwise and counter clockwise courses, and on the mighty climb to Pikes Peak. He achieved success at Indianapolis and at the Daytona 500, took top spoils at the Daytona and Sebring endurance events, conquering several championships and titles along the way. Finally, he is also the second American to win the Formula 1 World Championship. More importantly, as he took the checkered flag 111 times during a career that spanned four decades, he drove with joy and passion. This outstanding record elevated Mario Andretti to iconic status in racing history, making him an instantly recognizable figure throughout the world, as well as one of the most sought after and respected personalities in motorsport. Mario was born in the little town of Montona, Italy, on February 28, 1940, just a few months before the country was thrust into war. The Andretti family luckily survived the shattering afflictions of the time only to become refugees from Communism, spending several years in a camp in Tuscany as they patiently waited to immigrate to the United States. In 1954, Mario and twin brother Aldo found their way to Monza to watch the Italian Grand Prix. It was to be a stirring and inspiring experience for the youngsters as they rooted for their idol, the great Alberto Ascari. The following year, as their family settled in Nazareth, Pennsylvania, the boys were thrilled to discover a race track near their home, a half-mile oval used by modified stock cars. It was the perfect backdrop to set things in motion for the twins and put Mario on his winning road to the elite. Spirited drives quickly led him through the ranks of midget and sprint car racing, however an accident put a premature end to Aldo's career. Mario went on to win his first Indycar race in 1965 and became the youngest driver (at age 25) to be crowned champion in the series.

Ever since his memorable trip to Monza as a teenager, Mario had Grand Prix racing in his blood. During a fateful encounter at Indianapolis with legendary team owner Colin Chapman, he expressed his interest in driving a Formula 1 car someday, and Chapman replied, "Mario, whenever you're ready, just give me a call." He did just that a few years later. In 1968, Team Lotus entered Andretti in the US Grand Prix at Watkins Glen for a very promising, if abbreviated, debut. Although he had never driven at the Glen, he stunned the Formula 1

ABOVE LEFT: Mario Andretti at Watkins Glen in 1968 for his grand Formula 1 debut. The American proved his worth at the outset, putting his Lotus on pole and battling Stewart's Matra for the lead until a clutch failure put an end to his first Grand Prix.

Podiums	Fastest Laps	Points	Average Points/Race	Average Points/Season	Laps Led
18	10	180	1,41	12,86	798

fraternity by putting his Lotus-Ford on pole, the first ever F1 driver to do so in his first race. The following day, onlookers took further notice as he battled Jackie Stewart for the lead until mechanical problems thwarted his efforts. Reliability issues also dogged the three races he ran with Lotus in 1969, a season which saw him clinch his one and only victory in the Indy 500. In 1970, Andretti drove a March-Cosworth sponsored by STP's Andy Granatelli in five races, but only managed to finish once, placing third at the Spanish Grand Prix. Mario's fortunes in Formula 1 took a turn for the better in early 1971. While his priorities still lay with the US open-wheel scene, he struck a part-time deal with Ferrari to which he had delivered the manufacturer's only sportscar victory, at Sebring, the year before. In his first time out with the Scuderia, he won the South African Grand Prix, a triumph which naturally induced high emotions for the man who vividly remembered Ascari's own exploits with the prestigious Italian team. "Oh yeah" he recalled, "it was probably my biggest high, that very first Grand Prix win. And for Ferrari!" Quite remarkably, he followed this up with another victory in the scarlet red car, albeit in a non-championship event which took place at Ontario, California, where Formula 1 cars were pitted against F5000 machines. The remainder of '71 and the '72 season saw him compete in nine more

ABOVE: Friend and sponsor Andy Granatelli offers some advice to Andretti before the 1970 Spanish Grand Prix. RIGHT: Andretti heads to his first World Championship podium finish in his dirt-covered STP March at Jarama. FOLLOWING PAGE: A few weeks after clinching his first Formula 1 victory in South Africa in 1971, Andretti claimed another win with Ferrari, this time at the non-championship Questor Grand Prix which was held at Ontario, California.

"OH YEAH, IT WAS PROBABLY MY BIGGEST HIGH, THAT VERY FIRST GRAND PRIX WIN. AND FOR FERRARI."

Britax
5
STP

5
Shel

races for Ferrari with only mediocre results linked to the team's inability to provide a reliable machine. Andretti committed to Vel's Parnelli Jones promising Formula 1 effort for a full-time drive in 1975, but it was an unsatisfying stint in the underfunded team, whose driver struggled to make the graceful looking Parnelli competitive. The plug was finally pulled on the whole operation after the first few races of the '76 season, with Andretti migrating back to Lotus despite Chapman's team also facing a performance lull. Regardless, Mario was determined to pursue his dream of winning the World Championship as he viewed Chapman and his team's potential as intact. Their alliance would prove formidable but success did not come overnight and was not without tension, as Andretti once told *Motor Sports*' Nigel Roebuck: "When we first got together, Colin says, 'Mario, I always want to make a car as light as possible.' I said 'Well, Colin, I want to live as long as possible. I guess we need to talk.'" Andretti added, "Working with him was no trip to Paris but I guess you're always going to have problems with a genius, right? All in all, Colin was a wonderful chapter in my life--he was such a maverick." The pair captured their first victory together in the season finale in Japan where Mario lapped the field in torrential rain. In 1977, armed with the innovative Lotus 78, he earned seven poles and won four races en route to a third place finish in the driver standings, a clear shot at the title denied by several inopportune failures of Cosworth's development engines. Then

ABOVE: Andretti's stint with Vel's Parnelli Jones Racing was met with lackluster results in 1975 as low funding and a subsequent lack of development hindered the team's performance. RIGHT: Questor Grand Prix winner Mario Andretti displays his impressive trophy in victory lane.

"WORKING WITH CHAPMAN WAS NO TRIP TO PARIS, BUT I GUESS YOU'RE ALWAYS GOING TO HAVE PROBLEMS WITH A GENIUS, RIGHT"

STP
BELL

Chapman pulled the Lotus 79 wing-car out of his hat, the ultimate in ground-effects. From the Belgian Grand Prix at Zolder, where the car first appeared, Lotus and its drivers were simply in a league of their own, with Andretti claiming six wins and the coveted world title. Unfortunately, success was marred by tragedy when Ronnie Peterson, Mario's teammate and the only real opposition he faced that year, suffered critical injuries in a fiery crash soon after the start of the Italian Grand Prix at Monza. In a cruel twist of fate, as in the case of America's first World Champion, Phil Hill, what should have been Andretti's finest triumph was shattered by the death of his teammate. In retrospect, he had won the last Formula 1 race of his prolific career in the sandy dunes of Zandvoort that summer. The following two seasons saw Chapman and Andretti lose their winning way, plagued by mechanical problems, or simply overpowered and out-engineered by rival teams and their superior mastering of ground-effects technology. A switch to Alfa-Romeo in 1981 brought only three meager championship points in what was to be his last full-time stint as a Formula 1 driver. It was genuinely thought that Andretti's one-off with the Williams team at Long Beach in 1982, where he replaced the retired Carlos Reutemann, would be the final piece of the great American's period in Formula 1, but his final bravura performance fittingly took place at Monza, a track intimately linked to so many of his racing memories. When the call came from Ferrari to replace the injured Didier Pironi, Mario put the powerful turbo-charged 126 C2 on pole with typical gusto, a performance which naturally brought down the entire house of tifosi. The following day he scored his last championship points when he finished third. Two weeks later, in his Formula 1 swan song, Andretti started his last Grand Prix at Las Vegas, retiring early unfortunately after a mechanical failure.

His extraordinary time spent at the pinnacle of racing had produced 12 Grands Prix victories, 18 pole positions, 10 fastest laps and 799 laps in the lead in 128 race starts. Mario's coolness behind the wheel masked a fierce competitive spirit, even as he battled

LEFT: Andretti mastered torrential rain in Japan in 1976 to conquer his second Formula 1 triumph, and his first with Lotus. RIGHT: Chapman and Andretti on the winner's rostrum at Long Beach in 1977, celebrating one of their many victories together.

LEFT: Andretti leads teammate Ronnie Peterson at the Dutch Grand Prix at Zandvoort in 1978. Armed with Chapman's Lotus 79 'wing-car', the pair was dominant all year. Tragically, the great Swedish driver would die at the end of the season of injuries sustained in the Italian Grand Prix. Like Phil Hill 17 years earlier, Mario Andretti was crowned World Champion at Monza, in a race where he lost his teammate.

wheel-to-wheel in Indycars with his own son, Michael, in the latter stage of his career. Always respected as a driver and man, he was aggressive at 250 mph, but always fair. As one of the sport's greatest ambassadors, and the patriarchal figure of the family's racing dynasty, Mario remains vibrant and actively involved in motor racing today, working as a spokesperson, associate or friend to top executives around the world. Healthy and fit at 72, he could slip right back into the cockpit of a race car and indeed often does, driving IndyCar's two-seater which allows passengers to experience the speed and thrill that comes with an open-wheel racing machine.

A man of many interests, Mario still goes through life with the pedal to the metal. After measuring success in hundredths of a second, he has turned his attention to the slow art of making wine, a devoted passion which grew with his many travels to exotic places around the world. Nestled in the heart of Napa Valley, Andretti Winery was founded in 1996 and has consistently produced award winning wines. "My heart and soul are still in racing," Mario says, "and I still get real excited about new ventures, even Facebook and Twitter, but I just love when we release a new wine. There's nothing more delicate than your palate, so if I get a smile or a compliment on my wines, that's the ultimate satisfaction." Just like getting pole position in a Ferrari at Monza!

BELOW: In 1981, Mario drove for Alfa Romeo, scoring his only points of the season in the first race at Long Beach. RIGHT: In a fitting end to his F1 career, Andretti raced with Ferrari in the last two races of the 1982 season. At Monza, the scene of his first encounter with Grand Prix racing as a teenager in 1954, he put the beautiful 126 C2 on pole, in typical gusto.
The next day, Mario enjoyed a solid run to third place, scoring his ultimate championship points.

Marlboro
Intermedics
LONGINES
Agip
28
MAGNET MARELLI
olivetti

GRAND PRIX WINNERS

DAN GURNEY | RICHIE GINTHER | PETER REVSON

FLYING HIGH

DAN GURNEY

4 WINS

He was the best American road racer of his generation and the only competitor that Jim Clark truly feared. Dan Gurney never won the World Championship, but those who did considered the Californian very much their equal.

Before the overwhelming importance of commercial sponsorship in motor racing, back in the day when drivers were chosen by teams purely on merit, everyone pretty much got what they deserved over the course of a racing career. History offers its unfair share of injustices however, and Dan Gurney is widely regarded - along with Stirling Moss - as the most talented and worthy Grand Prix driver never to win the Formula 1 World Championship. In spite of this inequity, Gurney's impact on motorsports has been huge as a driver, team owner and manufacturer. And he has won races doing all at the same time. He won in sports cars, stock cars, Indy cars and in Grand Prix cars. Versatile as well as fast, he was the ultimate all-rounder, just as Mario Andretti would be later on.

Daniel Sexton Gurney was born April 13, 1930, in Port Jefferson, New York, the son of a Metropolitan Opera singer. However, the sound of a 12-cylinder engine was evidently sweeter to his ears than any voluptuous aria. Captured by the stories he read about exotic races in Europe and the heroes of the time, names like Caracciola, Rosemeyer or Nuvolari, his interest in racing and in anything that moved fast on wheels intensified. When his father retired, the family moved west and settled in Riverside, California, where he developed his driving skills by weaving through Southern California orange groves. After serving two years with the United States Army, part of which was spent in Korea, he resumed his racing aspirations in 1955, driving a Triumph TR2 in his first proper road race. Gurney then acquired a Porsche Speedster and made his breakthrough with remarkable ease in West Coast events, attracting the interest of several prominent sports car owners including Frank Arciero. In Arciero's Ferrari, Gurney finished a strong second to Carroll Shelby in the first quality international field he had ever faced. An attentive

ABOVE: In his second race with Ferrari in 1959, Gurney is pushed to the grid before the German Grand Prix at the Avus Ring where he would finish an impressive 2nd.

follower of Dan's impressive drives at that time was Luigi Chinetti, and just as he had done with Phil Hill a few years earlier, Chinetti arranged a Le Mans ride for Gurney while touting him to Enzo Ferrari.

Once Dan had his start in sports car racing with the Italian team, he wanted to move into Grand Prix racing. He got his ride in the 1959 French Grand Prix at Reims, where the 28 year-old rookie with only 20 race starts under his belt started his run up the Formula 1 ladder. "I was scared to death," Gurney admits, "twenty races and driving for Ferrari in Formula 1! I had almost given up and gone home at that stage, but Phil Hill helped a lot and encouraged me to hang on. When it finally did happen, it came with a giant rush, even though that first race ended after 20 laps with a pierced radiator." He finished second in his next start with the Scuderia, third in his third and fourth in his fourth. It was a remarkable debut, mocked by Gurney when he says, "I was going downhill fast! And never stopped." The lanky Californian thought he would get more consideration and understanding from an English-speaking team however, and left Ferrari to go to Britain and accept an offer from BRM for 1960. All he got was a headache in a season marred by retirements. He signed with Porsche the following year, achieving three second place finishes, losing by only a tenth of a second to Giancarlo Baghetti's Ferrari in France. A year later, this time at Rouen, he delivered the goods and clinched his first Grand Prix victory and the first for Porsche. "That was a lucky win," he recalls. "But sometimes it's better to be lucky than good. The car was down on horsepower and the leaders got away, but one-by-one they broke down or slowed, and I wound up a surprised and very happy winner."

In 1964, Gurney switched to Brabham for the following three seasons, scoring three podium finishes in his first year and rejoicing in the winner's circle once again at the French Grand Prix at Rouen, his second Formula 1 triumph and a historic first win for Jack Brabham's team. The Australian's engineering approach to racing was outstanding, but he also ran a very austere operation, which in some circumstances proved detrimental to the team's results. Spare parts were scarce, while mechanical troubles were often linked to five-and-dime items. At Spa that year, Gurney blasted off from pole and pulled out a huge lead when his Brabham began to run out of fuel in the closing laps. He pitted for help, only to find out that there was no fuel! He barely was able to hold on to sixth place. In the season-ending Mexican Grand Prix, Gurney's luck turned up for once as he inherited the lead from Clark and scored his third victory in Formula 1. Reliability problems and a lack of speed plagued the early part of Gurney's 1965 season while the Brabham - now shod on Goodyear tires - was sound and in contention in the second half of the year as Gurney collected five podium finishes and fourth in the World Championship standings. Blindingly fast when his mount was spared reliability issues, Dan's limited number of wins had evidently been a consequence of the cars he had driven than any measure of his talent. The frustrations associated with developing a new car were something that Gurney was very much aware of after his experiences with BRM, Porsche and Brabham. But the prospect of building and fielding his own machine - an American Grand Prix car - was simply irresistible in his view. Dan remembers the genesis of All American Racers he co-found with Carroll Shelby in 1965. "The opportunity came when Goodyear, who was fighting Firestone for supremacy at Indianapolis, asked me if I could set up a team of people to build a car for Indy. I said I could do it but that any effort would also have to include a Formula 1 car. Goodyear agreed and I felt it was just an opportunity that I had to take, even if the chances were slim." Lotus engineer Len Terry was entrusted with the design of the first Eagle Formula 1 car, while Weslake in England manufactured

LEFT: Gurney's Porsche leads Phil Hill at Monaco in 1961. ABOVE: Huschke von Hanstein, Ferry Porsche and Dan Gurney are all smiles before the 1962 German Grand Prix. RIGHT: Gurney rounds 'Nouveau Monde' at Rouen in 1962, on his way to his very first Grand Prix triumph.

"I WAS SCARED TO DEATH... TWENTY RACES AND DRIVING FOR FERRARI IN FORMULA 1!"

30

LEFT: Photographer Bernard Cahier surrounded by two of his favorite drivers, Gurney and Hill at Rouen in 1962. BELOW: Clark and Gurney battle at Zandvoort in 1964. RIGHT: Gurney and Bandini running nose to tail through Monza's Parabolica in 1965.

a 3.0 liter V-12 engine which complied with the new technical regulations that came into force in 1966. The Belgian Grand Prix marked the first appearance of the astonishingly beautiful dark-blue Eagle, with its distinctive bill-like nose, powered at first by an old Climax engine. At the following race at Reims, Gurney drove his car to fifth place, scoring the first World Championship points ever by an American Formula 1 car.

In 1967, equipped with the Weslake plant and featuring a lightened magnesium-titanium chassis, the Eagle started to fly. Gurney won the non-championship Race of Champions at Brands Hatch in March, but at Spa it all finally came together. Dan was fresh from his victory at Le Mans with Ford and AJ Foyt the previous weekend. "One of my better weeks at the office," as he likes to say. Despite a fuel pressure problem and a misfire which forced him into the pits at one stage, he took a resounding victory. "I even ended up getting the lap record," he recalls, "and at that time it was far and away the quickest F1 record. I must admit though that I wasn't all that confident when I was out up front. Because of the misfire, I was expecting the Weslake to expire at any time. I just gassed it and hoped for the best." Gurney's triumph put him in a league of his own, making him the only driver to take maiden World Championship race wins for three different constructors. It was a tremendous achievement for himself and the entire AAR team, and one which put Dan's own existence into perspective, as he remembers. "After the race, I got on to the plane and thought, 'Well I could crash now without any regrets as I've made it into the history books.'"

36

PREVIOUS PAGE: The Eagle flies through Eau Rouge at Spa as Gurney powers to a glorious win in the 1967 Belgian Grand Prix. RIGHT: Foyt and Gurney rejoice after the their victory at Le Mans in 1967. Gurney's success in the classic endurance event came just a week before his F1 win at Spa. "One of my better weeks at the office..", as he once said.
BELOW: America's legendary driver-constructors, Jim Hall and Dan Gurney.

Unfortunately, funding from Goodyear started to dry up and 1968 was an uneventful year for Gurney in Formula 1. The Italian Grand Prix at Monza was his last outing in the Eagle, and lasted only 19 laps. AAR's efforts in F1 had come to an end while its involvement in Indy cars was ramping up. Gurney scored his last championship points at Watkins Glen in 1968 driving a McLaren. In retrospect, the Californian's will to win under the star spangled banner may have cost him a World Championship, or even two, when one considers the titles won by Brabham in 1966 and 1967, but the man has no regrets. "We had an opportunity and we took it," he concludes. "We won two Formula 1 races and whipped the Ferrari factory, and then at Spa, we whipped them all. I look back at the whole Eagle experience as being more miraculous than it was disappointing."

By the time Dan Gurney had retired from racing in 1970, he had competed in 312 events in 20 countries with 51 different makes of cars winning 51 races, and 47 podiums. AAR's activities went into full gear after Dan's retirement, winning 8 championships and capturing 78 victories and 83 pole positions, including the Indy 500, the 12 hours of Sebring and 24 Hours of Daytona.

A member of various Motorsports Halls of Fame, Gurney has been a pioneer of racing innovations. In 1971 he developed the Gurney Flap (a small strip of material fit onto a car's aerodynamic wing), which has been adopted by the automobile racing industry throughout the world. He was the first race car driver

"WE WON TWO F1 RACES AND WHIPPED FERRARI, AND THEN AT SPA, WE WHIPPED THEM ALL."

to introduce the full-face Bell helmet to Indycar racing as well as Grand Prix racing. He was instrumental in launching the rear-engine revolution in Indianapolis in 1963 by bringing Ford and Lotus to the Speedway. His exuberant gesture of spraying champagne into the crowd from the victory podium at Le Mans over 45 years ago has been emulated worldwide by winners ever since. An avid reader of political and military history, Gurney loves old movies, opera, cigars, traveling to historical places and riding motorcycles. Gurney and his wife, Evi, who was a junior executive in the public relations/press department of Porsche in Stuttgart and a well-known motorsports journalist in Germany during the sixties, have been married since 1969. They have two sons. Dan has four children from his first marriage and has eight grandchildren. At the funeral of the late Jimmy Clark, who was killed at Hockenheim in 1968, the great Scotsman's father took Dan aside at one point and said to him, "Jimmy always told me that you were the only driver he really feared in a race car." Could there have been a more fitting compliment paid to the incredible talent of Daniel Sexton Gurney?

LEFT: Gurney wound-up his F1 career with Team McLaren in 1970. Here, at Clermont Ferrand, he debriefs with team manager Teddy Mayer while chief mechanic Tyler Alexander works in the background.

TRUE GRIT

RICHIE GINTHER

1 WIN

An improbable racing journey took Richie Ginther to places he never expected to go. From wrenching cars in Los Angeles to driving for Ferrari in Europe, his career followed an itinerary guided by an outstanding talent and one very big heart.

As accurate as they may be, statistics only offer a shallow perception of reality, void of any substance or specifics. A glance at Richie Ginther's career reveals just a single Grand Prix win, albeit a historic one as the driver's personal milestone achieved at Mexico in 1965 delivered both Honda and Goodyear's first triumph in Formula 1. What the numbers will never disclose however, is that Ginther was a formidable opponent to the European aces during the '60s, and to fellow Americans Phil Hill and Dan Gurney. They show no evidence of his outstanding skills as a development and test driver, and they offer no testimony to the fact that he was a 'racer' at heart. Inspired solely by a passion for the engineering and performance of the cars he drove, indisposed to motor racing's ever increasing commercialism, Ginther was a purist.

Born in Los Angeles in 1930, Paul Richard Ginther was trained in motor engineering and rapidly earned a reputation as a clever and meticulous mechanic. His friendship with Phil Hill encouraged the diminutive, freckled-faced Californian to take up racing himself, which he did with a hybrid Ford-powered MG TC in 1951. Two years in the army as an aircraft mechanic in Korea kept him off the tracks until 1953, when he was recruited by Hill as his riding mechanic in the grueling Carrera Panamericana. In 1955, he was back behind the wheel, racing various machines for the dealership that employed him but his big break came when VW/Porsche dealer Johnny von Neumann provided Ginther with a Porsche Spyder, and he became a force to be reckoned with in West Coast events. He made his first trip to Europe in 1957, driving a Ferrari at Le Mans for Luigi Chinetti.

Enzo Ferrari was well disposed towards American drivers at the time as he felt that this encouraged sales of his cars in the US. With a little help from Phil Hill and Chinetti, Ginther was contracted to the Scuderia in 1960 and given the task of testing and developing the team's sportscar and Formula 1 machines. "That was Richie's thing," Phil Hill once said. "He just loved to stay out there and grind around all winter long and to fiddle with this, that, and the other to develop those cars." Ginther was entrusted with an experimental mid-engine Ferrari at Monaco for his first Grand Prix, producing a remarkable time in qualifying which equaled Hill's and securing his very first World Championship point with a

ABOVE: Ginther rounds the old Station Hairpin in his Ferrari 156, en route to a second place finish behind Stirling Moss in the 1961 Monaco Grand Prix

sixth place finish. He repeated the feat at Zandvoort, this time with the front-engine Dino 246, and was runner-up to his victorious team mate at Monza. Ginther was made a full-time member of the Italian squad in 1961, driving the new and highly efficient 156 'Sharknose'. His finest drive that season - and perhaps the best of his career- came in the streets of Monte Carlo. Ginther powered off the front row of the grid and led for 13 laps before being passed by Hill and Bonnier, but he was back in second place by lap 75. He then set off in pursuit of the flying Stirling Moss, and indeed almost caught the maestro, finishing just a few seconds adrift. While many often considered Ginther's charge at Monaco in 1961 as his finest moment, years later, his own view on the subject appeared tainted with displeasure as he felt he had been held back that day by Phil Hill. Seeking a better appreciation of his talent, he defected to BRM in 1962 only to find himself once again playing second fiddle to a Hill, this time Graham Hill. Good results were a rarity in his first season with the British team although things did improve in 1963 when he was on the podium more often than not, flanked on the upper step by his World Champion team mate. The opportunity to join Honda as its number one driver in 1965 brought the ultimate prize: a Grand Prix victory. In spite of a season centered on the competitive development of the team's troublesome RA272 chassis/engine combination, Ginther emerged victorious in the final round at Mexico. It proved to be his only Formula 1 win, but a landmark event nevertheless as the triumph was also a historic first for Honda and Goodyear.

Ginther ran only a handful of races in 1966 before walking away from the sport while attempting to qualify for the Indy 500 in 1967, shaken by an accident and tired of all the politics. He may only have a single Grand Prix win to his credit, he nevertheless achieved 14 podiums and scored 107 championship points, and was considered by many on the brink of greatness. Richie eventually retired with his wife, Cleo, to a quiet home on the Baja Peninsula. In 1989, he was reunited with one of his BRM Grand Prix cars at Donington on the occasion of the marque's 40th anniversary. In typical Ginther fashion, and in spite of his precarious health, he drove it hard and fast. A few days later, while vacationing in France, Richie Ginther died of heart failure at the age of 59.

LEFT: Ginther battling with his Ferrari mount at a very wet British Grand Prix at Aintree in 1961.
ABOVE and RIGHT: The Californian's landmark victory in Mexico in 1965 was the high point of his career. It was also a historic first for Honda and Goodyear.

HE DEFECTED TO BRM ONLY TO FIND HIMSELF ONCE AGAIN PLAYING SECOND FIDDLE TO A HILL. THIS TIME GRAHAM HILL.

IN HIS OWN WAY

PETER REVSON

2 WINS

It was a long and winding road to the top for Peter Revson. But once he got there, he established himself as a respected winner. And then came the spring of 1974.

One may wonder what compulsion drives an individual to motor racing's ragged edge. Why would a smart, well-educated young man, whose prosperous family could have sent him on the easy road to life wish to make a living confronting fear and mortality? For much of his career, Peter Revson was a continuous target of such speculation. Yes, there was the Revlon connection, but contrary to tabloid belief, he was not a heir to the cosmetics group's fortune; Revlon was owned by his uncle. Charles Revson. His Hollywood good looks and well-groomed charm only reinforced the misguided image of a dashing hobby-driver playboy. Anyone foolish enough to slap a 'heir' label on Revson's back or question his dedication and commitment as a professional racing driver, and do it to his face, was greeted with a mighty stare of contempt and a few unequivocal words to go with it. The truth is: Peter Revson paid his own way to the top of the sport, earning the respect and admiration of his peers.

Born in New York in 1939, Peter's education involved Eastern prep schools and universities. His racing aspirations started in Hawaii (where his mother had moved) in 1961 when he took his Morgan Plus 4 to a win in an SCCA club event in his second race. As Revson became progressively more involved in racing he acquired a Cooper Formula Junior in 1962, partnering with Teddy and Timmy Mayer, as they formed the Rev-Em Formula Junior team. Revson then used $ 12,000 of his own savings – acquired after a brief and unrewarding stint at an advertising agency on Madison Avenue – to move to England in 1963. Campaigning his privately-entered little Cooper around the European continent, Revson was aided by a single mechanic and lived out of the back of an old bread van. It was somewhat of a Bohemian life for the young aspiring champion, but nevertheless fueled his dreams and ambitions, as he once recalled : "I remember sitting on the beach at Monte Carlo and looking up at the Hotel de Paris, saying to myself 'I'll be sleeping there one day'".

Revson's rise to prominence in Grand Prix racing was a two-part story, the first of which took place during the swinging sixties and was marked by relative chaos. His stock had appreciated enough to gain him his first Formula 1 ride in 1964 when an independent Reg Parnell-run Lotus-BRM was entered in a couple of

ABOVE: Peter Revson survived a first lap pile-up and a re-start to capture his long-awaited inaugural Grand Prix win at Silverstone in 1973. FOLLOWING PAGE: In his debut season with McLaren, Revson proved consistent and fast. At Brands Hatch in 1972, he collected his second podium finish of the year.

Player Specials
REVSON
YARDLEY
GOODYEAR
YARDLEY
19
GOOD/YEAR

YARDLEY
GOODYEAR

non-championship races and six World Championship events. No significant results were achieved through that effort so he took a pragmatic step back in 1965, running in F2 and F3, and winning impressively the latter formula's coveted Grand Prix of Monaco, an achievement which provided a timely boost to his prestige. During this trying period, Revson lived in London, sharing an apartment with fellow racers Chris Amon and Mike Hailwood. "We were known as the Ditton Road flyers," Peter once recalled. "And some wild parties went on in that little flat. At the time, Chris was already getting rides that any driver would have groveled for, while Mike was the hottest thing on two wheels in Europe. As for myself, I knew that if I was going to stay in racing, I had to make it pay. My old man was secretly hoping I'd fail and return home and do something sane and safe. I damn near did, but then I thought of that ad agency..."

Revson did return home at the end of the '65 season, only to take his racing and skills to the next level as he drove for Ford in their GT40s and mighty Can-Am cars. The summer of 1967 was marked by a personal loss for Peter when his brother Doug, who was also trying to make a name for himself in racing, was killed in an obscure F3 race in Denmark. The fatality did nothing to dampen his ambitions although it further reinforced the strained relationship with his family who opposed his racing aspirations. Revson was a non-qualifier at Indy in 1967 but finished a creditable 5th at the Brickyard in 1969 with a Brabham after starting dead last. That achievement got the attention of McLaren who called upon the rising star the following year to replace an uncompetitive Chris Amon. His name was finally top of the bill in 1971 when he set a new qualifying record and bagged pole position for the Indy 500, finishing second with his McLaren-Offy. His Can-Am season was even better, as he took five wins in the series and was crowned champion. The end of the '71 season also saw a return to F1 when Ken Tyrrell provided Revson with a one-off drive at Watkins Glen. His US GP was over after just a single lap when the Tyrrell-Cosworth lost its clutch.

Peter Revson had undoubtedly blossomed as a professional race driver, and his rise to the big time had nothing to do with wealth, good looks, or social status. More importantly, his all-around performances got him back to where he once belonged: Grand Prix racing. Team McLaren headman and old buddy Teddy Mayer signed Revson to race in 1972 alongside former World Champion Denny Hulme. With four podium finishes and one pole position, he enjoyed an impressive first year, ending up fifth in the championship although his USAC Indycar commitments with McLaren had forced him to miss three races. The following season got off to a rocky start but once Revson was armed with the rapid Gordon Coppuck-designed McLaren M23, he was running with the leaders. The high point came at Silverstone where 'Revvie' scored his first Grand Prix victory, and the fifth for an American driver in F1. The field had been seriously depleted after a huge first lap pile-up caused by his team mate, Jody Scheckter. On the restart, Revson came through and delivered the goods. At the

"MY OLD MAN WAS SECRETLY HOPING I'D FAIL AND RETURN HOME... I DAMN NEAR DID, BUT THEN I THOUGHT OF THAT AD AGENCY..."

Canadian GP at Mosport, he again beat the field to conquer his second F1 victory, although chaotic circumstances, marked by rain, tire stops, a pace car and countless lead changes, put the final race result in jeopardy for several hours as officials studied the lap charts.

In spite of a great year and another fifth place in the standings, tensions were brewing between Revson and Mayer. When it came to arrangements for the 1974 season, those who held the sponsorship monies – Marlboro and Texaco – dictated their requirements. Revson was offered a drive in a third McLaren, again run under the Yardley banner, but declined to be exiled to a team which he thought would not receive the proper effort and support. He signed for Don Nichols' UOP Shadow team, and committed himself to developing the new DN3 car with the intent of taking the American team up the ladder of success. Unfortunately, only three races into the year, while testing at Kyalami just a week before the South African Grand Prix, a suspension failure violently pitched the sleek black racer into the barrier, fatally injuring its driver. Peter Revson was 35. Revson's tragic death saddened immensely those who had followed his achievements over the years and watched as he refined his talent and skills through commitment and dedication. "I really feel Peter was one of the top 6 drivers in F1," Teddy Mayer once said. "He had a burning desire to succeed and confound those who doubted his motivation. He believed that just because someone walks around with a famous name doesn't mean there isn't any hard work involved. He rose to the top, and he did it on his own, in his way."

LEFT: From the outset of the 1974 season, Revson was committed to taking Shadow up the ladder of success. The South American races revealed a promising potential, but it would all go terribly wrong at Kyalami. RIGHT: Joan Cahier is just as thrilled as Revson after the American's inaugural Grand Prix win at Silverstone.

ON THE PODIUM

ARRY SCHELL | MASTEN GREGORY | MARK DONOHUE | GEORGE FOLLMER | EDDIE CHEEVER | MICHAEL ANDRETTI

AS THE HANDSOME SCHELL'S REPUTATION AS A DRIVER GREW, SO DID HIS FAME AS A COLORFUL WOMANIZER.

HARRY SCHELL

2 PODIUMS

Likeable Harry Schell never won a Grand Prix, but Formula 1's most flamboyant character did enjoy his fair share of glory.

Harry Schell was the son of American expatriates living in Europe. His existence was only declared to authorities in 1921, when the US embassy in Paris reopened after the first World War, and although he never admitted to the fact, many in Formula 1 believed he was much older than what his passport asserted ! In any case, he is inscribed in history as America's first representative in post-war Grand Prix racing, even though he only visited the US for the first time in 1940. Schell's parents were both heavily involved in racing, managing their own team known as Ecurie Bleue. When his father was killed in an accident, Harry followed his mother back to the United States and to the Indy 500 where he witnessed his first major motor racing event before joining the US Army and reportedly being stationed, albeit briefly, in Monte-Carlo of all places. After the war, Schell stayed in Europe and put his racing heritage to good use in the late 1940s, tackling a few Grands Prix and Formula 2 events with a Cooper.

As the handsome and stylish Harry Schell's reputation as a driver grew, so did his fame as a colorful womanizer. His was a popular figure amongst his peers, who enjoyed his sense of humor and jovial approach to life's pleasure. Schell's career gathered momentum at the inception of the F1 World Championship in 1950 with some spirited drives on board Maseratis, Gordinis and

LEFT: Harry Schell at Reims in 1958 driving his Owen Racing Organisation BRM.

Vanwalls. He scored his first championship point in Argentina in 1954 and collected his initial podium finish at Pescara in 1957, achieving a career-best second place at Zandvoort with the factory supported BRM team in 1958. Schell's finest drive was actually a 'did-not-finish' at Reims in the 1956 French Grand Prix. In that race, he replaced an ill Mike Hawthron after his own Vanwall had gone out earlier with an engine failure. He stunned the crowd when he charged from eighth place to catch the leading Ferraris of Fangio and Castelotti before a fuel-injection problem forced him out of the race.

Over the course of his ten year term in F1, Schell raced more different cars and for more teams than any other American Grand Prix driver. It's also worth noting that he was also the first driver to race a mid-engine machine in a World Championship event when he started the Monaco Grand Prix with his Cooper-Jap in 1950. "There's no question Harry had talent," acknowledged close friend Carroll Shelby. "He was fast and could lead races, but he was old. Maybe ten years older than what he admitted to! So he didn't have a lot of stamina and had difficulty remaining consistent over the duration of a race. But he was a real character and so much fun to be with. He was also one hell of a practical joker, so you always had to watch your back with Harry." One of Schell's most memorable pranks led to perhaps his greatest moment. At Sebring in 1959, he achieved the best qualifying performance of his career when he put his Cooper on the front row of the US GP. Schell's lap was a massive six seconds faster than his previous best performance around the old airfield, to the complete bewilderment of his fellow competitors, as Phil Hill once remembered. "He cheated! Harry took advantage of an unmanned marshal's post around the back of the track to take a crafty short cut! He said it was just a joke but he told the marshals nothing about it, and when the cars lined up on the grid, there he was, being wheeled onto the front row, with a huge smile on his face."

Harry Schell's prospects began to dim at the end of the Fifties. In 1960, he decided to campaign a private Cooper under the revived Ecurie Bleue family banner. Unfortunately, Argentina would be the American pioneer's last Grand Prix. At Silverstone a few months later, while practicing for the non-championship International Trophy event, he lost control of his Cooper in the rain at Abbey Curve and crashed into a barrier. He became the first American to die in F1. Grand Prix racing lost a free-spirit and a great character.

MASTEN GREGORY

3 PODIUMS

t was often said that Masten Gregory vas blind as a bat without his glasses, ut blindingly fast with them. His track ecord fails to reflect his outstanding alent as a driver.

ports car legend Carroll Shelby always thought the hort, slight-built, bespectacled Masten Gregory had n abundance of talent. "Man, those glasses were as nick as Coke bottles," the Texan once said. "But he vas the fastest American that ever went over to drive a rand Prix car. Hell, he scored more points than nyone did in their first year!" One might also add that e did it while only competing in four of the eight World hampionship races which took place in 1957. he youngest of three children whose parents owned an insurance company in Kansas City, Masten Gregory kick started his career in 1951 when a substantial inheritance was made available to him by his mother. He wasted no time in acquiring a Mercury-powered Allard sports car, taking his first win in his third race! He then graduated to a Jaguar C-Type, successfully showcasing his indisputable talent in numerous SCCA events. His wins and growing reputation earned him an invitation to race in his first international sports car event

ABOVE: After winning a sportscar race at the Nürburgring, Masten Gregory receives a mark of affection from the wife of German ace Rudolf Caracciola.
FAR LEFT: Gregory's Maserati 250F races up a hill on the picturesque Pescara circuit in Italy in 1957. LEFT: The bespectacled Gregory at the 'Ring in a BRM in 1965.

EARLY ON IN HIS CAREER, GREGORY HAD DEVELOPPED A TALENT OF A DIFFERENT SORT: THE HIGH-SPEED BAILOUT!

in Buenos Aires in 1953. The following years were marked by drives in a variety of machines, including a 3-liter Ferrari at Le Mans and a Porsche 550 Spyder which he shared with Carroll Shelby, to take a class win in the Tourist Trophy race at Dunrod.

In 1957, he traveled once again to South America and took top honors with three other drivers in the Argentine 1000 km sports car race. The event preceded the Buenos Aires Grand Prix where the who's who of racing took notice of the American's efforts and skills behind the wheel. Highly impressed, Mimo Dei, the headman of Scuderia Centro Sud, offered Gregory his first World Championship Grand Prix start at Monaco. Without the slightest inhibition or constraint, the freshman put in an impressive drive to third place around the twisty and demanding street course, becoming the first American in the history of F1 to score a debut podium finish. He followed up this performance with an eighth place finish in the German Grand Prix at the Nürburgring, a fourth place finish at Pescara, and another fourth place finish in the season-ending Italian GP at Monza, rewarding himself with sixth place in the World Championship.

Early in his career, Gregory had also developed a talent of a different sort: the high-speed bailout! A maneuver which consisted of standing up on the seat of his moving car, whenever a crash loomed ever larger and jumping ship before the impact! Unfortunately, a chronic injury sustained on one such occasion hampered his 1958 season, which was perhaps for the better as the Maserati 250F was past its prime anyway. There was an opportunity to shine in 1959 when Cooper contracted his services to race alongside Jack Brabham. A podium finish at Zandvoort was followed by a retirement in France, where Gregory had been forced to stop because of exhaustion while he was running second. In Portugal, a strong drive to second preceded Gregory's discharge from the British team. He was replaced by the young Bruce McLaren; a strange fate for a man whose performances were gaining momentum. Many believed that politics had soured his relationship with Cooper as the American was simply faster than team mate Brabham. So the latter had him fired! Had this not been the case, Masten Grgeory may well have been the first American to win an F1 race.

From 1960 to his ultimate season in Formula 1 in 1965, Gregory never really got the machinery his outstanding talent and commitment deserved, although there were odd flashes of greatness. The US Grand Prix at Watkins Glen in 1962, where he finished sixth with an independently-run UDT Laystall Lotus, would prove to be his last points-scoring Grand Prix. Fortunately, Masten's woes in F1 were somewhat counterbalanced by a distinguished career in sports car racing, the culmination of which was a triumph with Jochen Rindt in a Ferrari 250 LM at Le Mans in 1965. Gregory retired from racing in 1972, affected (as much) by the death that year at Le Mans of his good friend Jo Bonnier and his own close calls.. The 'Kansas City Flash', passed away from a heart attack in his apartment in Porto Ercole, Italy in 1985.

LEFT: In 1965, Masten Gregory entered four World Championship events with a Scuderia Centro Sud BRM. He is pictured here on his way to 8th place in the German Grand Prix. ABOVE: The great Fangio pays a visit to Gregory in Argentina in 1960.

PENSKE AND DONOHUE DID THINGS WITH CARS THAT OTHER DRIVERS SIMPLY COULD NOT WRAP THEIR MIND AROUND.

MARK DONOHUE

1 PODIUM

To a generation of fans in the 1960s and '70s, Mark Donohue's outstanding career is so intimately linked to Penske Racing that any attempt to focus exclusively on the history of one would only diminish the merits of the other.

Mark Donohue was a fast and smart driver. Together with his engineering background and unique talent for setting up a car, his association with Roger Penske elevated technical sophistication and preparation to levels never seen before. As a team, the pair did things with cars that other drivers simply could not wrap their mind around. From sports cars, Trans-Am or Can-Am to the Indianapolis 500, the well chronicled triumphs and performances of the Donohue-Penske duo embodied an elegant style as much as a unique spirit in American motor racing, where nothing was left to chance, before or after a race. Such a formidable partnership just had to tackle Formula1, and Donohue's first foray into the Grand Prix arena took place at the end of 1971 season when Penske entered a semi-works McLaren M19A in the Canadian Grand Prix at Mosport. Starting eighth on the grid the dark blue Sunoco-sponsored machine was fourth after a single lap, finishing a tremendous third, with Donohue the only driver on the same lap as winner Stewart and runner-up Peterson. Two weeks later at the Glen, a practice accident sidelined Mark for the US Grand Prix. It was expected the team would capitalize on its impressive F1 debut but Penske's priorities lay with winning the Indy 500, which was duly accomplished in 1972. Donohue's Can-Am duties were hampered by a huge crash and a broken leg later that year but he was back behind the wheel in 1973, capturing the title in the overpowering Porsche 917/30 before announcing his retirement from the sport with the intention of taking up a managerial role at Penske. But for Roger, as much as for Mark, Formula 1 was unfinished business and a worthy challenge. So the team decided to field its own car, and no driver was better suited to develop and race it than Donohue. The Penske PC1 ran for the first time in 1974, in the season ending North American races, but without working any miracles. In 1975, as the team took part in its first full F1 campaign, the PC1's development was so troublesome that the car was canned altogether and replaced by a customer March 751 chassis. The change proved opportune when team and driver were rewarded with a fifth place finish at Silverstone and two World Championship points. A month later, during the pre-race warm-up before the Austrian Grand Prix at Zeltweg, a right front tire blew causing the March to hit the Armco at high speed and flip over the barrier, the car destroyed but its driver emerging relatively unscathed. Later that day, Donohue complained of a worsening headache only to be diagnosed with a blood clot in the brain. An operation appeared successful, but Mark then slipped into a coma and died two days later, his wife Eden by his side.

No matter how extraordinary a driver he had been, friends and colleagues remembered Mark Donohue most for his sportsmanship, intelligence and kindness. Roger Penske offered his own tribute to his driver's legacy. "Mark obviously was a key to Penske Racing's early successes. He became a great friend of mine, and he committed his life to auto racing. Mark obviously brought an air of professionalism. I think the people at Indy thought we were the college guys with the crew haircuts and the polished wheels. We used to clean our garage out every night, and that was something people didn't understand. I think at that point we started to bring the sport to a higher level; we brought some technology. We started to look at data; Mark was an engineer from Brown University, and certainly that was part of it. But we were committed. We weren't out there to have fun – we were there to go racing." And go racing they did.

LEFT: Mark Donohue and Roger Penske formed a formidable racing partnership. The pair was unrivaled when it came to race car preparation and technical excellence, working with the greatest commitment as they sought their 'unfair advantage'. ABOVE: Donohue in the Penske PC1 at Anderstorp in 1975.

GEORGE WASN'T OVER THE HILL WHEN HE MADE HIS GRAND PRIX DEBUT, BUT HE WAS NO SPRING CHICKEN EITHER.

GEORGE FOLLMER

1 PODIUM

George Follmer was a talented all-rounder, as versatile as they come, who competed in virtually every form of auto racing, and won at most.

Born in Phoenix in 1934, he was rather late to the game when he started racing in his mid-20s, turning pro in 1965 when he won the SCCA's United States Road Racing Championship with a tiny under-two-liter Lotus 23 powered by a Porsche 904 engine. His success encouraged him to relinquish his job as an insurance salesman and focus full-time on racing as he moved on to big-bore machines entered in the colorful Trans-Am and Can-Am series. In 1972, he actually became the first and only driver to collect the title trophy in both championships, achieving four wins with Roy Woods Javelin and five victories in Roger Penske's mighty turbo-charged Porsche 917 10K.

George wasn't over the hill when he made his Grand Prix debut in 1973 at 39 years old, but he was no spring chicken. He had signed for Don Nichols' new UOP Shadow team to race in the World Championship alongside Jackie Oliver, and while the prospect of tackling F1 without any relevant single-seater experience appears daunting, he acquitted himself superbly in the first three races he entered. This, in spite of the elegant black Shadow DN1 penned by British designer Tony Southgate not even turning a wheel before it arrived in South Africa for the third round of the championship. "We finished those cars in Kyalami," Follmer said in Tim Considine's great book '*American Grand Prix*'. "They were shipped straight from England to South Africa, and that's where we finished them and ran them. It was one of those things where you just go out

and run. I didn't have any problem with it." Oliver's machine retired early on but Follmer drove a steady race from 21st on the grid all the way to sixth, collecting a point in his first Grand Prix. He repeated that result a month later in the non-championship International Trophy event at Silverstone, and then scored a remarkable third place podium finish at the Spanish GP in Barcelona after a couple of spirited battles with Ickx and Revson. Follmer's reputation of a tough and difficult driver to overtake also came to light at that race when a heated debate flared up on the podium with second placed-man François Cevert. "You bet I was difficult to get by," George remembered. "I guess he just wanted me to pull over and get out of the way. Yeah, good luck with that!"

Unfortunately, the remarkable string of results achieved at those first three races would prove to be the crescendo of Follmer's Grand Prix career. Reliability issues and an altogether underperforming machine undermined Shadow's initial year in F1, to the American driver's detriment. "Yeah, there were good finishes in the beginning. But we had a lot of teething problems within the team because it was new. Then it fell apart. There was also a bunch of friction between Oliver and myself, and the team was basically run by Oliver. He called the shots, ego got into play, and I didn't get the cars, the engines. That's the way it goes."

Stateside, Follmer resumed his versatile role as a leading contender in Nascar, Trans-Am and IMSA until a stuck throttle in a Can-Am race at Laguna Seca in 1978 led to disaster. A broken leg and damage to his spine ended his professional career. George was inducted into the Motorsports Hall of Fame in 1999. In 2012, he was the recipient of the Phil Hill Award, an honor bestowed upon him by the Road Racing Drivers Club for his outstanding service to road racing. At 78, he's still a frequent participant in vintage events, and make no mistake about it, George Follmer is as tough behind the wheel as in the good old days!

LEFT: In only his second Grand Prix, George Follmer brought his Shadow home to a fine third place finish in Spain in 1973. The performance would prove to be the American's best result in Formula 1.

CHEEVER WAS PERCEIVED AS SUCH A GREAT TALENT THAT EVEN FERRARI COURTED THE 19-YEAR OLD.

EDDIE CHEEVER

9 PODIUMS

Eddie Cheever's path to the pinnacle of racing followed a decisively un-American way. The roots of his passion were not to be found in sprint cars, dirt tracks or any other form of US motor sport, but under the traditional routes of European road racing.

Although he was born in Phoenix, Eddie Cheever grew up in Rome, Italy where his parents had opened a chain of health clubs. He began racing karts at the age of 13 and the action-packed, wheel-to-wheel battles in the nimble little machines, where he fought against future F1 rivals Riccardo Patrese and Elio de Angeles, fueled his ambitions from the start. At 16, he seamlessly graduated to cars, moving up the junior formulae ranks at a blistering pace. In 1977, he was perceived as such a great talent that Ferrari courted the 19 year-old for a full-fledged works drive in F1 the following year. In the end however, it would be another prodigy – Gilles Villeneuve – who would inherit that prime spot.

It was a clumsy first step up the Grand Prix ladder as his first outings resulted in two non-qualifications with the low-budget Theodore racing team and a lackluster one-off with Hesketh Racing. A tad unprepared for the big time, Cheever retreated to F2 with the Osella team in 1979 and then followed the small Italian squad back into F1 for his first full season, albeit one which was dogged by poor reliability and performance. Always the talent-spotter, Ken Tyrrell offered Eddie a better environment in which to learn his trade. In 1981, the American scored his first championship points at Long Beach in his first race with the British team. He would enjoy four more top-six finishes that year in the Tyrrell Cosworth. Now a firmly established member of the F1 fraternity, Cheever switched to the French Ligier team for '82, racing alongside Jacques Laffite and achieved his first of three podiums that season at the Belgian GP at Zolder. The engaging role of 'An American in Paris' was quite enjoyable to Cheever whose fortunes rose considerably when he was chosen to partner Alain Prost in the factory Renault team in 1983. Armed with the mighty power of the car's V6 turbo-charged engine, he was a regular top-ten contender in qualifying all season but reliability issues undermined his efforts in half of the races. He nevertheless secured three thirds: in France, Belgium and Italy, and one second in Canada, the highlight of his year.

In retrospect, there had been no shortage of commitment, enthusiasm or talent on Cheever's part, as he showed finesse and skill, especially on streets circuits. However, playing a supporting role to Prost's championship bid, or being compared to the phenomenal Frenchman and future four-time World Champion, probably weakened Eddie's achievements and perhaps convinced Renault not to renew his contract for the following season. Cheever found refuge with the Benetton-Alfa Romeo squad for 1984 and 1985, but there was only a single points finish (ironically in his first race with the team). In the two lean years he was there, driving a car powered by a thirsty and very unreliable Alfa V8, he lost his momentum. Eddie Cheever was out of F1 in 1986 – apart from a guest outing for the Haas-Lola team in Detroit – before returning for a three-year stint with Arrows. A few points and two podium finishes were all the lanky driver was awarded in that period. His final year of Grand Prix racing was particularly painful; literally, as Cheever composed with the low line Arrows A11 in which he barely fit. In spite of often enduring cutting agony in the machine's cramped cockpit, he set it all aside in his home town of Phoenix in 1989 when he enjoyed an emotional run to third and his last

LEFT: Detroit's Renaissance Center offers its spectacular scenery to Eddie Cheever and the Renault team in 1983.

E.CHEEVER
25

podium finish in F1. For many, Cheever's time at the top had been marked by a potential never realized. True, he rarely disposed of machinery worthy of his ability, and when he did, bad luck or mechanical failures were the norm rather than the exception. In all fairness, there were also clear traits of inconsistency in his performances; a spirited drive was often followed in the next race by an anonymous mid-field run. In the end, Eddie Cheever holds the record for achieving more Grand Prix starts – 132 – than any other American driver in history. Life after F1 brought Cheever success in sports cars with the TWR-Jaguar team before he carved out a niche for himself in Indycar racing, becoming one of the most popular drivers within the IRL community. In 1998, after setting up his own team, Eddie Cheever took the biggest prize of his career when he won the Indy 500 from 17th position on the grid.

LEFT: Cheever's Matra-powered Ligier at full speed at Monza in 1982. ABOVE: Eddie ended his F1 career with a four-year spell with Arrows.

Marlboro
KENWOOD
BERLUCCHI
BERLUCCHI
Marlboro
7
COURTAULDS
Shell
GOODYEAR
Ford

MICHAEL ANDRETTI

1 PODIUM

An impressive genetic inheritance awarded Michael Andretti a head start in motor racing, but when it came to Formula 1, bad timing and some faulty decisions sealed his fate.

Success in F1 is never guaranteed. It's a high-powered world, strewn with pitfalls and traps, where talent is significant but ineffective without a strong mind and the commitment to galvanize a team towards the common goal of victory. To that end, timing in F1 is paramount. For many, Michael Andretti's foray into Grand Prix racing in 1993 was all about being in the right place at the wrong time. As the dominant IndyCar driver of the early 1990s, Michael's credentials were outstanding. His speed, race craft and fearless late-braking made him a racer's racer, with 27 wins to his name and the 1991 CART championship under his belt. In short, he was the real deal. No American driver seemed better prepared to represent the US in F1 since his legendary father won the World Championship in 1978. McLaren boss Ron Dennis knew it. In early 1991, he had offered Andretti an opportunity to sample the world of F1 at Estoril, and although it was only a 12-lap session, the test initiated Dennis' careful supervising of the young driver's progress. A year later, McLaren was facing a difficult season on all levels: performance was under par (by McLaren standards), the team was set to lose its Honda engine supply, and its star driver, Ayrton Senna, was talking about packing it in and moving to arch-rival Williams-Renault. Ron Dennis was in urgent need of some substance. In September 1992, he flew to Detroit and signed Michael Andretti to drive for McLaren in 1993. "I think he can be a Grand Prix winner," Dennis said at the press conference, "and in the process of winning he can become the World Champion. It's not a question of which country you come from. It's how best you demonstrate that desire to win. And Michael has that desire."

LEFT: After a season of mishaps and disappointments from both driver and team in 1993, Michael Andretti ended his Grand Prix career at Monza with a scintillating drive to third place. Alas, it was too little too late for the talented Indycar driver.

Unfortunately, Michael's year ended with the first piece of bad news. McLaren had been hopeful of securing Renault power for 1993, but the agreement failed to materialize, forcing it to sign a Ford customer deal, giving the team second billing after the manufacturer's works contract with Benetton. Soon after, more trouble hit the wires when FISA – the sport's governing authority – ruled that in-season testing would be limited to a track in a team's home country. More importantly, there would also be a limit on the number of tires available during race weekends, as well as limits to the number of laps a driver could do. As a result, Andretti would be deprived of crucial track time and imposed a learning curve steeper than initially anticipated. When the light turned green in South Africa for the first race of the year, the atmosphere surrounding Michael Andretti was highly-charged, and the pressure was on. Senna was there, offering as much advice and assistance to his novice team mate as he could; it could not have been a more disastrous start to a F1 driver's career. In his first three Formula 1 races Michael failed to complete the first lap with the rest of the field even once. His car stalled on the grid at Kyalami, and when he finally did get moving he collided with another driver after four laps. In Brazil, he locked wheels with Gerhard Berger's Ferrari on the run down to the first corner, catapulting himself into the air and writing off the McLaren in the process. A few weeks later at Donington, another collision on the opening lap put him into the gravel trap and out of contention. At that point, Michael Andretti's season appeared to be following the painful rules of Murphy's Law. Scattered signs of progress brought a couple of points in Spain and another in France, but by mid-season, doubts

IN HIS LAST TWO HOURS OF FORMULA 1, MICHAEL RACED WITH HIS OWN FLAIR, AS COMMITTED AS EVER…

vere cast on his ability to measure up and perform at he highest level. Errors of judgment resulted in contacts, spins and early retirements which opened ew cracks in Michael's confidence.

Questions emerged about Andretti's sense of commit-nent as the team watched its driver pop in for race veekends and then commute back across the Atlantic o Pennsylvania, instead of taking up residence a tone's throw from the factory, where he could be alled upon at a few hours notice for testing. Young McLaren test driver Mika Häkkinen, who was waiting n the wings and closely watching Andretti's situation evolve - or rather dissolve, was offered significant rack time in the American's absence, and he put that nileage to good use. Slowly, perception became reality at McLaren as sentiment towards Michael shifted from patience and leniency to outright rejection. It almost became a game of hoping he would fail.

And then there was also the case of Michael's hen-wife, Sandy, whose ever-presence in the McLaren pit, coupled with her loud and lavish accou-rements and veneration for the limelight, were just oo much for the mild-mannered, muted-colored eam. Regardless of what anyone thought, Michael vas very much a distant number two driver at McLaren, perceived from within as 'a kid with a amous name, who raced in that lesser formula back n the States'; a flash in the pan, who was no Senna. Nothing could have been further from the truth.

To a certain extent, circumstances conspired to under-mine Andretti's efforts and indisputable talent. He was simply given a raw deal. The underpowered McLaren-Ford MP 4/8 was no world-beater, something even Senna acknowledged, while a cap on practice and quali-ying laps complicated the task of learning on the job. True, if Andretti had camped outside the team's factory n Woking or relentlessly grinded around the race track at every scheduled test session, it would have improved his status and his consistency in terms of performance. To that, both critics and supporters seem to admit. Another reality is often overlooked however: McLaren was in a bad year, and as history would prove, in the early stages of a multi-year cycle of underperformance. With the writing on the wall, Michael Andretti lined up on a F1 grid for the last time at Monza, where his father had clinched the World Championship in 1978, and where Phil Hill had done the same in 1961. In his last two hours of F1, he raced with his own flair, as commit-ted as ever, charging back from 20th after a spin and a pit stop on the second lap to a splendid third place podium finish, his best Grand Prix result. It was too little too late. Michael was out, permanently, and Häkkinen was in for the last three races of the season.

F1's cut-throat, all-or-nothing world takes no prisoners. Circumstances, inexperience, the errors to which he readily admitted and dark side politics combined to turn Michael Andretti's dream into a nightmare. "Honestly, between the time when I signed that deal with McLaren and when we started the season, many things changed, and not for the better," Michael reflects. "That said, I'll admit I should have been better prepared before starting my first Grand Prix, because everything just snowballed and really hurt my confidence and the team's confidence. But at one stage, I was making progress, and had I been given a chance, a real chance, and another year, I guarantee that I would have lived up to those expectations, and the end result would have been a lot different. Unfortunately, it will always remain unfinished business for me and the worst experience in my racing career."

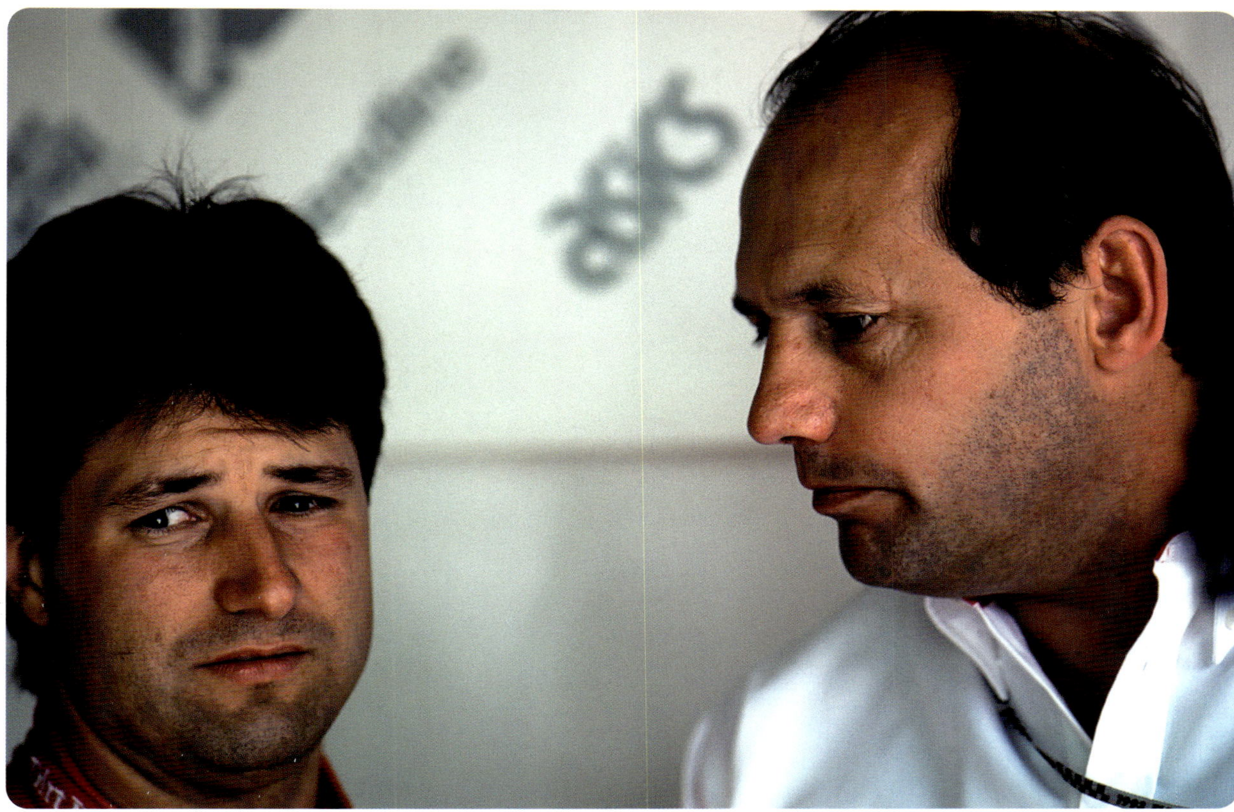

ABOVE: Hailed as a natural born winner when he arrived at McLaren, Michael was progressively rejected by Ron Dennis as the season wore on. Circumstances, mistakes and a mutually shattered confidence combined to strain the pair's working relationship.

IN THE POINTS

M HALL | WALT HANSGEN | RONNIE BUCKNUM | BOB BONDURANT | DANNY SULLIVAN

D A
12

JIM HALL

3 POINTS

He took a shot at Grand Prix racing in 1963, but Jim Hall's calling was with the big-bore machines back home.

As the creator of the extraordinary lineage of Chaparral cars, Jim Hall is a Texas legend. The remarkable technology achievements he pioneered, which amazed the world of sports car racing, often incite us to overlook the fact that Jim was not only a genius designer and successful car-owner, but also a fine racing driver. Born in Abilene, Texas, into a wealthy oil family, Jim showed an early interest in fast cars. He was drawn to racing while studying mechanical engineering at the California Institute of Technology, driving in his first race in 1954 with his brother's Austin Healey. Like many young drivers of his era, Jim Hall first made a name for himself in SCCA racing, competing in a variety of cars.

His success eventually led him to rent a private Lotus 18 for the 1960 United States Grand Prix at Riverside. It was an impressive debut as the novice driver ran as high as fifth before gearbox trouble put him out on the final lap. The following year, Hall tried F1 again, this time at Watkins Glen where the Lotus Climax retired after a fuel leak. It's worth noting that the 1961 US Grand Prix that year featured no less than eight American drivers. In addition to Hall, the grid included Dan Gurney, Roger Penske, Hap Sharp, Masten Gregory, Lloyd Ruby and Walt Hansgen. In 1962, Hall started his career as a prolific manufacturer when he set up Chaparral Cars Inc. with partner Hap Sharp. It wasn't long before the first mid-engine innovative design roared out of the Midland workshop, with many more to follow over the years. Hall nevertheless found the time to commit to a full season of Grand Prix racing in 1963, running in a British Racing Partnership Lotus 24 powered by a BRM engine. He scored championship points at the British and German Grands Prix. Hall was particularly proud of the result he achieved at the Nürburgring, one of the most demanding tracks in motor racing. In preparation for the race there, he spent the entire week hurling his little Mini Cooper S around the daunting circuit, trying to learn its 177 turns. Hall vividly remembers: "Yeah, I just grinded around all week long. But after all that practice, when I got into my race car, I was in for a big surprise. Because of the height you're sitting at, your eye-height, and the speed, the place looked completely different. I had to relearn the whole thing!" Fortunately, Jim also got some precious pointers from fellow racers Dan Gurney, Phil Hill and Richie Ginther. "They were in a black Mercedes," he recalls, "and they asked me if I wanted to join them for a few laps. I got to see each one of them drive a lap, look at their lines or where they put the car. That was a real lesson and pretty exciting." In the race, Hall's Lotus was never passed, Jim achieving a fifth place finish and his best result in a World Championship round.

At the end of the 1963 season, Jim Hall decided not to return to Grand Prix racing. A contributing factor was the fact that he simply felt more competitive racing the big bore engines he loved so much back home, rather than the small displacement machines associated with Formula 1. The promising race debut of the first Chaparral he designed encouraged Hall to focus exclusively on manufacturing and racing his innovative creations. This choice brought him great fulfillment and outstanding triumphs.

If one could rewrite history, it would have been fascinating to see Jim Hall apply his exceptional engineering acumen to the world of Formula 1. The developments his wizardry produced in the field of aerodynamics, ground effects, aluminum engine blocks or automatic transmissions would have been hailed as breakthrough technologies long before the advent of Colin Chapman's Lotus 78 or Gordon Murray's Brabham BT46 "fan car". If anyone ever tells you that Formula 1 has always been the most technologically advanced form of racing, tell them about the accomplishments of one Texas roadrunner named Jim Hall.

LEFT: At Silverstone in 1963, Jim Hall scored his first championship point driving a British Racing Partnership Lotus-BRM. The Texan quit Formula 1 at the end of the season and returned home to drive the big bore racing machines he loved so much. As the creator of Chaparral, his engineering genius earned him widespread acclaim.

WALT HANSGEN

2 POINTS

A meteoric rise through the ranks of sports cars and single-seaters carried Walt Hansgen to the highest level of racing in America and in Europe.

Born in New Jersey, Walt Hansgen was another driver who was a product of the SCCA sports car scene, rising through the series' ranks in the East Coast region. After racing Jaguars for a couple of years with great effectiveness, Walt was noticed by famed team owner Briggs Cunningham, and along with mechanic Alfred Momo the trio became a dominant force in regional road racing, setting the standard in both performance and machine preparation.

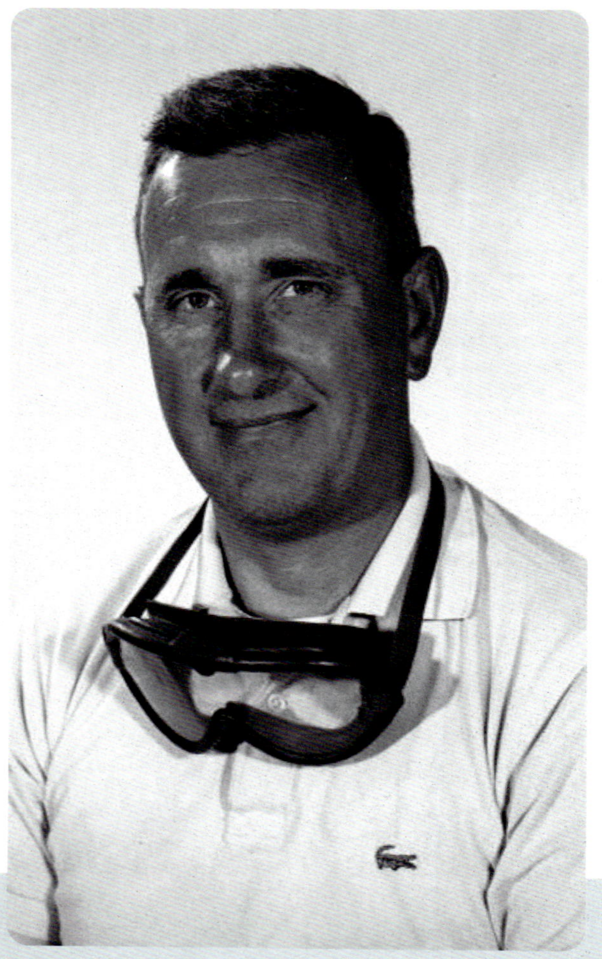

Hansgen enjoyed a few race wins in England before returning Stateside to start racing open-wheelers, eventually posting the first win by a Formula Junior car in America when he triumphed at Watkins Glen in 1959. His ongoing success led to an opportunity to race in Formula 1 in 1961 when Cunningham entered a Cooper in the United States Grand Prix. He qualified 14th but was forced out of the race while trying to avoid the spinning Lotus of Belgian driver Oliver Gendebien. A year later he was back in F1, racing a Lotus-Climax at the non-championship Mexican Grand Prix in which he retired with mechanical trouble.

In the following seasons, Hansgen drove a variety of cars for Cunningham and John Mecom, running as high as second in his MG-Liquid Suspension Special at the 1964 Indy 500 until an engine problem forced him to slow. Later that year, he was once again back in action in his home Grand Prix at the Glen, achieving a points scoring fifth place finish at the wheel of a Lotus Climax. There would be no more Formula 1 races for Hansgen after the Glen.

Walt remained a force to be reckoned with in sports car racing, also acting during this period as a mentor for a young rising star by the name of Mark Donohue. Included in Holman & Moody's line-up for Le Mans in 1966, Walt Hansgen was testing at the French track when his Ford GT 40 Mark II crashed in the rain at the end of the pit straight, leaving no chance of survival for the 47 year-old driver.

ABOVE: In one of his brief F1 appearances, Walt Hansgen entered his ex-works Lotus 18 in the non-championship Mexican Grand Prix in 1962.

RONNIE BUCKNUM

2 POINTS

Fewer drivers experienced a more unusual and surprising entry into Formula 1 than Ronnie Bucknum.

Ronnie Bucknum enjoyed considerable success campaigning an Austin Healey and an MG-B in the early '60s on the West Coast, establishing a name for himself and an impressive track record in the regional SCCA series. His credentials were promising, but they still appeared meager to justify a graduation overnight to fully fledged Grand Prix driver status. That is exactly what happened however, much to the bewilderment of the chosen one himself, as Bucknum recounted. "A guy from Honda had seen me race at Sebring, and a few days later I got a phone call from their American representative who said they wanted me to test their new Formula 1 car! I thought it was a joke and I went to a meeting expecting to be stood up. A short time later, I was on a flight to Japan."

BELOW: Bucknum in the Honda RA271 at Watkins Glen in 1964. Given his complete lack of open-wheel racing experience, the Californian appeared as a surprising choice when he was recruited by the Japanese manufacturer. Honda wished to enter the big time without raising any undue expectations.

The fact that Ronnie had never even sat in an open-wheel race car, let alone raced one, appeared to be of no importance to Honda, who itself was just starting to manufacture road cars, its commercial success centered exclusively around motorcycles up to that point. Perhaps the driver's lack of an international racing pedigree was a prerequisite for the Japanese so they could then test and race their machine without raising undue expectations. Initially, Yoshio Nakamura, the man responsible for Honda's Formula 1 efforts, wanted the company to act merely as an engine supplier to a confirmed team. A partnership was agreed to with Colin Chapman for Honda's radical 1,500cc transverse V-12 to power Jimmy Clark's Lotus in 1964, but Chapman reneged on the deal, a turnabout which infuriated Nakamura, forcing the manufacturer to build its own F1 chassis. The first Honda Formula 1 car was rolled out at the German Grand Prix in the summer of '64, with team and driver both thrown in at the deep end of Grand Prix racing on the daunting Nürburgring. Bucknum, as talented as he may have been, certainly had his work cut out for him. Testing prior to the race had been limited, while a visit to the British Grand Prix a few weeks earlier was his first encounter with Formula 1 as well as his first trip to Europe. Given the circumstances and the teething problems associated with any new racing car, Ronnie acquitted himself well, starting last but overtaking a few drivers and lasting 12 of the 15 laps before steering problems put him out of the race. At Monza a month later, he ran as high as seventh before the engine overheated. His performance encouraged Honda to keep him on a team which added fellow-Californian Richie Ginther to its formation in 1965. "Richie's arrival was a real bonus," Ronnie remembered. "His development skills improved the car dramatically and we really thought we had a winner on our hands."

Unfortunately, another steering failure during a pre-season test in Japan sent Bucknum into the barriers. A broken leg deprived him of precious track time and relegated his status to a clear number two to Ginther.

When the '65 season got underway, the first four races were met with an equal number of retirements while tension also grew between Bucknum and his high-strung team mate. After the French Grand Prix at Clermont-Ferrand and another poor showing by both drivers, Ginther convinced Honda to concentrate on only one car, his, until reliability issues could be sorted out. "Yeah, I was out of the car for the next three races but when I came back at Monza, I qualified in front of Richie, which was some consolation." In the last race of the '65 season, at Mexico, Ronnie Bucknum scored his only championship points with a fifth place finish in a race which saw the mercurial Ginther provide Honda with its first Grand Prix victory. The following year ushered in a new era for Formula 1 with its 3-litre engine regulation, and Bucknum was called upon by Honda to race in the end-of-season US and Mexican races, his last efforts in F1.

His motor racing career continued as he raced on in sports cars, Can-Am and in USAC. Ronnie Bucknum died in 1962 at the comparatively young age of 57, from complications linked to diabetes. His son Jeff embarked on his own racing career, competing in sports and GT cars as well as in the Indy Racing League in 2005.

ABOVE: In an attempt to overcome the language barrier which existed between himself and his Honda engineers, Bucknum resorted to means of communication which involved a lot of gesturing and drawing.
RIGHT: Bucknum in Mexico in 1965. On race day, Ginther convinced Honda to switch cars with his team mate, powering himself to victory in the superior machine while Bucknum finished a distant 5th.

THE FACT THAT RONNIE HAD NEVER EVEN SAT IN AN OPEN-WHEEL RACE CAR WAS OF NO IMPORTANCE TO HONDA.

12
18

"MY FIRST GRAND PRIX, AND I WAS IN A FERRARI!"

BOB BONDURANT

3 POINTS

Few drivers enjoyed the privilege of making their grand Formula 1 debut with the Scuderia Ferrari. Bob Bondurant was one of them.

Born in Illinois, Bob Bondurant grew up in Los Angeles and like so many drivers of the '50s and '60s, he cut his teeth on the West Coast sports car scene. His winning ways, achieved mainly in a variety of Corvettes, galvanized his ambitions and reputation, attracting the interest of Carroll Shelby who included Bondurant in his Ford Cobra team. In 1964, he was off to Europe, winning the GT class at Le Mans before conquering the FIA World Manufacturer's Championship in 1965 with the all American squad, taking victory in seven of the ten races. Bondurant's skills did not go unnoticed. Ferrari in particular showed a keen interest in the man who had inflicted defeat upon the mighty Italian squad in the manufacturer's championship. At the request of works Ferrari driver John Surtees, a visit to Maranello was scheduled just before the 1965 Italian Grand Prix at Monza. Bondurant was offered a guided tour of the manufacturer's facilities by Enzo Ferrari himself, where much to the driver's delight, the prospect of a sports car drive with the Scuderia was also discussed. A few weeks later, Surtees broke a leg in a Can-Am race at Mosport and Bob was called upon to replace the British driver in the prestigious red scarlet team for the United States Grand Prix at Watkins Glen. It would prove to be a memorable debut, although not exactly for the right reasons as Bondurant vividly recalled. "My first Grand Prix, and I was in a Ferrari! I started 13th and worked my way up to sixth, but when it began to rain, the elastic strap on my goggles started to stretch and they blew down on my face. I couldn't see anything! I couldn't come in to the pits because I would have lost too much time, so I had to pull them back up and hold them, putting my knee against the wheel and shifting with my right hand. I still ended up ninth. I felt great, and the car - they gave me the V8 - was just fantastic." Bob only enjoyed one ride with Ferrari but three weeks later he got another crack at Formula 1. "I went down to Mexico just to watch, but with my helmet and bag, just in case. As it turned out Innes Ireland failed to show up on time to drive Reg Parnell's Lotus-BRM. Reg fired him on the spot and put me in the car. In the race, it was really working good until a tie-rod broke and put me out."

LEFT: Bob Bondurant is eyes wide open at Monaco in 1966. A solid drive in his Team Chamaco-Collect BRM earned him a 4th place finish.

Bob Bondurant signed on with Team Chamaco Collect for five races in 1966, driving a private BRM powered by a two-litre engine while most of the other teams had upgraded to the eligible new three-litre motors. At Monaco, on a track he knew well, having raced there in Formula 3, he put in a strong drive from last on the grid to fourth place, scoring three championship points. Unfortunately, it was all downhill after that as the team and its under qualified staff just weren't up to F1 standards. Bob's ultimate rides at the pinnacle of racing were with Dan Gurney's Eagle team at Watkins Glen and Mexico. "I always liked racing F1 and I would have liked to have stayed on with Gurney because I knew I could do well. But Dan felt he needed Richie Ginther to help him sort the cars because Richie was good at that. It just didn't work out in the end."

Bob pursued his racing ambitions on other fronts, eventually putting his expertise to use for the benefit of others when he created the "Bob Bondurant School of High Performance Driving" in 1968. Forty-four years later, time permitting, he continues to teach driving and car control at the institution's state of the art training facility at Firebird Raceway in Phoenix, Arizona.

SULLIVAN HOUNDED DOWN ROSBERG AND GAVE THE FINN AN EXCITING RUN FOR HIS MONEY.

DANNY SULLIVAN

2 POINTS

This Kentucky kid's effort in Formula 1 was not without merit, and should have produced another season of Grand Prix racing.

Whenever racing enthusiasts talk about Danny Sullivan, you can be sure they'll mention the driver's moment of glory at the Indianapolis 500 in 1985; not the overwhelming instant when he took the checkered flag, and not the emotional jubilation as he sipped the winner's milk in Victory Lane. What will be remembered is the foolish mistake he made on lap 120, when he lost it out of Turn 1 while taking the lead from Mario Andretti, snapped into a monumental spin and got away with it! Sullivan not only recovered from the mishap, twenty laps later he tried the move again. This time it worked, and he went on to conquer one of the most famous victories in the history of the Indy 500, known as the "Spin and Win."

Born in Kentucky, Danny Sullivan's career started in Europe where he attended the notorious Jim Russell Racing Driver's School at Snetterton before scrapping through the open-wheel road racing ranks in the late 1970s. With the support of affluent whiskey magnate Garvin Brown, he won races in the SCCA Can-AM series in the early 1980s and made his Indycar debut in 1982 with an impressive third place finish at Atlanta. Always on the lookout for new talent, Ken Tyrrell invited Sullivan to a private Formula 1 test at the Paul Ricard circuit in Southern France along with ten other drivers at the end of 1982, and then gave the American another opportunity to shine in Brazil during a pre-season test a few months later. When the 1983 season got underway in Rio de Janeiro,

Danny Sullivan was a fully-fledged Grand Prix driver with Tyrrell, running alongside in-form Michele Alboreto, who was fresh from victory in the last race of 1982 in Las Vegas. The personable driver's good looks and attractive style were a perfect match on the commercial side for the team's new sponsor, the Benetton clothing company, making its landmark entry into Formula 1. Eleventh in Brazil was followed by an upbeat ninth place on the grid at Long Beach and a run to eighth in the race. Danny's next outing came at the non-championship Race of Champions at Brands Hatch, in which a limited number of teams competed to gain some extra mileage before the

LEFT: Danny Sullivan showed evident potential in his one year apprenticeship in F1 with Ken Tyrrell in 1983. In the end though, the Kentucky kid would find his calling in Indycar racing.

European leg of the season got underway. It was the last non-championship F1 race to be held in the sport's history and proved to be the highlight of Sullivan's career in Grand Prix racing. The sole Tyrrell driver in the field, he put in a remarkable effort, hounding down the Williams of leader Keke Rosberg and sitting on his tail for the last fifteen laps, unable to get past but giving the Finn an exciting run for his money. All year long, the normally-aspirated Tyrrells and their drivers were forced to play second fiddle to the mighty turbo machines, and as a consequence, Sullivan's results were lackluster. He did however score two championship points, finishing fifth at Monaco after starting last on a track where the Cosworth engine's drivability reduced the car's disadvantage. Tyrrell received an upgrade from its engine supplier towards the end of the season, and Sullivan made good use of the extra power by out qualifying the experienced Alboreto in two of the last three races. At Kyalami, in the ultimate round of the championship, and in his last F1 ride, he put in a spirited drive from last to seventh. "Yeah, that was a good race," the American remembers. "The car had a last-minute problem on the grid and by the time I got started, they were gone! The normally-aspirated engines were way down on power there because of the altitude at Johannesburg, so I really had to put in a charge. Ken was impressed."

Despite ending the year on a solid performance, Sullivan decided to return stateside and commit to Doug Shierson's Indycar team. "It wasn't an easy decision because Ken wanted me to stay on, but without a turbo, what was the point ? I wanted to win and the prospects in Indycar were simply better from that standpoint. In fact, I won three races in 1984 and the following year, we won Indy with Penske."

MAKING THE GRID

FITCH | WACKER | SHELBY | RUTTMAN | WARD | REVENTLOW | DAIGH | SHARP | RUBY | PENSKE
MAYER | SETTEMBER | LOVELY | BARBER | POSEY | LUNGER | ONGAIS | RAHAL | SPEED

Barred by a lack of desire or victims of unfavorable timing or circumstances, those who made up the numbers, as talented as they were, did not find their calling in Formula 1. They do deserve recognition and merit however, not for the mere fact that they raced with the best, but because they did not succumb to the greater risk of never to have tried.

MAKING THE GRID

JOHN FITCH

Born in Indianapolis, John Fitch was a Mustang P-51 fighter pilot in World War II before he started racing automobiles. As one of America's first postwar drivers to race successfully in Europe, he enjoyed an outstanding career which spanned 18 years. In the 1950s, he collected major sports car and class wins in the Grand Prix of Argentina, the Mille Miglia, the Tourist Trophy and Sebring. He also competed six times at Le Mans, running with Briggs Cunningham and, especially, with the mighty Mercedes-Benz team alongside legendary drivers Juan Manuel Fangio, Stirling Moss and Karl Kling. During this prosperous period, John Fitch entered two rounds of the Formula 1 World Championship, racing an HWM at Monza in 1953 and a Stirling Moss-owned Maserati 250 F at the same venue in 1955. A pioneer in racing, Fitch - whose ancestor John Fitch invented the steamship - was also at the forefront of road safety, developing the Fitch Barrier, a sand-filled plastic-barrel crash cushion that is commonly seen in front of bridge abutments. After officially retiring from racing in 1966, John Fitch returned to active duty at 87 years of age in 2004 when he was once again teamed up with a 50 year old Mercedes-Benz 300 SLR at Bonneville Salt Flats in an attempt to break a class land speed record. The extraordinary event is profiled in a visually striking documentary, "Gullwing at Twilight: The Bonneville Ride of John Fitch", which is occasionally aired on PBS.

FRED WACKER

A founding member and president of the Chicago branch of the Sports Car Club of America, Fred Wacker was a prominent businessman who extended his engineering interests beyond the two automotive companies he founded. He was first active in the Midwest and on the East Coast, successfully racing an Allard-Caddy in the late 1940s before travelling to Europe in 1951 to contest Le Mans for the Cunningham team. On his second trip to France in 1953, Wacker acquired a Gordini which he tested at the Montlhéry race track located on the outskirts of Paris. There and then, he discovered for the very first time the intricacies of driving an open-wheel single-seat race car, the little Grand Prix machine a far cry from anything he had driven before. His Formula 1 World Championship debut occurred later on that year at Spa where he brought the under-powered machine home to a ninth place finish. A huge accident during qualifying for the Swiss Grand Prix at Bremgarten spelled an end to Wacker's season but he was back in 1954 with the Gordini, retiring in Switzerland but finishing a creditable 6th in the Italian Grand Prix at Monza. Unfortunately, no championship points were awarded in those days for a sixth place finish. Wacker's burgeoning companies back in the United States eventually convinced him to abandon his racing aspirations and focus on his businesses, which he did with great success.

LEFT: Pictured here at the Italian Grand Prix at Monza in 1953, John Fitch was one of America's first post-war Formula 1 drivers. ABOVE RIGHT: Fred Wacker prepares to race his Gordini at Monza in 1954.

CARROLL SHELBY

If there was ever a man who could tame a snake, it was Carroll Shelby. The tough Texan farmer turned driver, manufacturer and entrepreneur, may have raced in only eight Grands Prix, his name will forever be known among racing enthusiasts as the man who created the Cobra and helped Ford beat Ferrari at Le Mans. As such, his legacy deserves more than just a statistical mention.

Shelby enjoyed a distinguished career in sports car racing in the mid-fifties, driving cars of various makes and engine size in the US, with a few forays overseas, notably with Aston Martin. In 1958, the British manufacturer's team manager, the great John Wyer, recruited Shelby for its booming sports car program in Europe. While racing on the Continent, his reputation earned him a drive in four Grands Prix with the independant Scuderia Centro Sud's Maserati 250F. Shelby manhandled the outdated machine to the best of his ability, achieving a fourth place finish in a car shared with Masten Gregory at the Italian Grand Prix at Monza. His close relationship with Aston Martin fueled his desire to drive the manufacturer's new F1 car in 1959. Unfortunately, the potential shown by the beautiful DBR4 when it was first wheeled out and tested just vanished as the season wore on. "It really wasn't worth a shit," Shelby remembered in his typical no-nonsense talk. "At Silverstone, we were right up there with the best, and then it kept going down on horsepower all year. The more they worked on it, the worse it got. I have no idea what the hell happened."

At the end of the 1959 season, the plug was pulled on Shelby and Aston Martin's efforts in F1. The team nevertheless rejoiced in their resounding victory that summer in the 24 Hours of Le Mans where the American shared the winning DBR1/300 with fellow Aston stalwart Roy Salvadori. Diagnosed with a heart murmur when he was 10, Shelby saw his condition worsen at the start of 1960. In spite of driving with nitroglycerin pills under his tongue, he decided to call it a day and retired from racing at the end of that year. His drive and ambition were intact though as he embarked on a career as an entrepreneur, realizing his dream of manufacturing a high-performance American sports car with the support of Ford. The legend of the Cobra was born, and led to outstanding success on and away from the race track. With Dan Gurney, he co-founded All American Racers which would field several Indy 500 winners and America's first victorious Grand Prix car. He was instrumental in guiding the development program of the Ford GT40 and its conquest of Le Mans. He helped Ford create the Shelby Mustang, and served as a performance consultant for Chrysler and its Dodge Viper. But perhaps the venture his was most proud of was the creation of the Carroll Shelby Foundation in 1992, dedicated to providing medical assistance to children in need. Carroll Shelby passed away on May 10th 2012, a extraordinary life fulfilled and accomplished

ABOVE: Carroll Shelby's Aston Martin leads David Piper's Lotus at Aintree in 1959. RIGHT: Shelby, Hill and Troy Ruttman share a laugh with Scuderia Centro Sud's Mimmo Dei at Reims in 1958.

DIAGNOSED WITH A HEART MURMUR WHEN HE WAS 10, SHELBY RACED WITH NITROGLYCERIN PILLS UNDER HIS TONGUE.

TROY RUTTMAN

The youngest ever winner of the Indy 500 in 1952 at the age of 22, Troy Ruttman was considered a prodigy, one of the most gifted drivers of his generation. Although a speedway specialist, his performance on road tracks attested to his outstanding natural ability. Ruttman's only Grand Prix start came at the French round of the World Championship, at Reims in 1958. Racing an old Maserati 250 F, he finished 10th in a race marked by the death of Ferrari driver Luigi Musso and Juan Manuel Fangio's last appearance in a Grand Prix. Another ride was scheduled at the Nürburgring two weeks later but a seized engine during practice forced the American to the sidelines for the race. "I enjoyed Formula 1," Ruttman recalled in Tim Considine's work *American Grand Prix Racing*. "But the way it appeared to me back then was that any equipment that one of us were going to get would be a hand-me-down from someone else. Also, I was having some personal problems right then, so it just didn't work out for me. A while later, I decided that was it and came home." Troy Ruttman retired from racing in 1964, after an ultimate run in the Indy 500.

RODGER WARD

A true superstar of American racing's golden age, Rodger Ward was one of the greatest drivers in Indianapolis 500 history. During a stretch between 1959 and 1964, he never finished worse than fourth, his victories achieved in 1959 and 1962. Born in Kansas, his family moved to Los Angeles where Roger was introduced to the local hot rod scene in the 1930s, building his own Ford-powered machine when he was just 14 years old. At the outset of World War II, he took to the skies, flying a P-38 fighter and then a B-17 bomber, his outstanding skills ultimately earning him a role as an instructor. After his discharge, Ward began his rise to stardom, racing midgets with considerable success as well as stock cars in the early 1950s, and also qualifying for his first Indy 500 in 1951. His first toe-in-the-water of Grand Prix racing was an over-zealous attempt to challenge the Formula 1 front-runners at Sebring in 1959 when he decided his Kurtis Kraft sprint car could perhaps measure up against the European machines and their drivers which, although a tactical misjudgment, was certainly a testimony to his boldness and determination. On a grid which included no less than seven American drivers, Ward was last, his qualifying time some 43 seconds off the pace of the Cooper Climax of poleman Stirling Moss. Ward's efforts behind the wheel of the Midget were fruitless but surely spectacular as he drifted his way around the airfields bumpy turns. Attrition pushed him up to eighth at one point but a clutch failure forced him out after 20 laps. Four years later, in 1963, he once again lined up on the grid of the US Grand Prix, this time at Watkins Glen where he rented Reg Parnell-run Lotus-BRM, a proper Formula 1 car, albeit one with considerable mileage. Gearbox problems put him out of contention after 44 laps. "It was a real eye opener for me in terms of skill required to drive those cars," Ward once admitted. "I enjoyed that race and really gained a lot of respect for the guys running in Formula 1. It whetted my appetite, but I realized by then, I was a little old to make a trek to Europe."

LANCE REVENTLOW

Alongside those who often endured a precarious existence before successfully rising through the ranks of Formula 1, there were others who simply had the money, if not the talent, to become Grand Prix drivers, adding to the sport's color and glamour. Lance Reventlow figured among the latter group, but displayed undisputable skill behind the wheel of the cars he raced. Reventlow was the only child of Woolworth heiress Barbara Hutton and Danish nobleman Count Curt von Haugwitz-Hardenberg-Reventlow. He was also the stepson of actor Cary Grant. As a teenager, his money afforded him the luxury to indulge in his passion for exotic sports cars which led to his involvement in motor racing. After competing in various club events around the Los Angeles area in the mid-fifties, often accompanied by his good friend James Dean, Lance eventually decided to go to Europe and spend a season racing a Cooper Formula 2. Upon his return to the States he set up a company to build his own all-American sports cars, called Scarabs, which enjoyed a fair amount of success. Reventlow then decided to embark on an ambitious project to field a front-

LEFT and ABOVE: Lance Reventlow and Chuch Daigh endured a difficult time in Europe in 1960. The Scarab was immaculately prepared, but completely out of date compared to its contemporary front-engine Formula 1 counterparts.

engine roadster in Formula 1 alongside hired driver and resident engineer Chuck Daigh. Unfortunately, Reventlow's effort was fruitless in the only race he ran, the Belgian Grand Prix at Spa in 1960, where he qualified 16th and retired after a single lap with a blown engine. Thrown in at the deep end and highly uncomfortable racing on the daunting Ardennes track, it was thought that the young millionaire purposely over-revved the motor, putting himself and the Scarab out of its misery. Only aged 25, he progressively lost interest in racing and returned to his prosperous life as heir and socialite. Lance Reventlow died in 1972 when his Cessna flew into a blind canyon in Colorado.

CHUCK DAIGH

"There are only two people I can think of who could sit down, take a welding torch, build their own chassis, go out to test it, and then win races with it. They are Jack Brabham and Chuck Daigh. I put Chuck in the same category as Jack." The high praise comes from one Carroll Shelby. Although Chuck Daigh never achieved star status in motor racing, there is no question that his competence in understanding and improving the inner workings of a racing car were matched by his

REVENTLOW'S MONEY AFFORDED HIM THE LUXURY TO INDULGE IN HIS PASSION FOR EXOTIC SPORTS CARS AND RACING.

ability to drive its wheels off. Success during the golden age of sports car racing on the West Coast led to Chuck's association with Lance Reventlow's Scarab team in 1957 and his introduction into Formula 1 in 1960. He took part in three Grands Prix that year, retiring the recalcitrant Scarab at Spa, but bringing home the ill-handling machine to a tenth place finish at Riverside. A one-off outing in a Cooper at Silverstone a few months before had also resulted in an early retirement. Chuck Daigh continued to race on in the early 1960s, mainly in sports cars. He passed away, after a brief illness in April 2008.

BELOW: Hap Sharp in Reg Parnell's Lotus 24 at the 1963 Mexican Grand Prix.

HAP SHARP

As a Texas oil man turned racer, it only seemed fitting for James "Hap" Sharp to team up with fellow Texan Jim Hall to form the company which would design and manufacture the successful Chaparral sports cars during the early and mid-1960s. Indeed, they won several races together, their finest hour - or rather 12 hours - coming at Sebring in 1965. Sharp ran his own Cooper Climax in the 1961 and 1962 US Grand Prix, qualifying fairly well but finishing down the order. He contested the end-of-season US and Mexican Grand Prix in 1963 in a Reg Parnell Racing Lotus BRM, placing seventh in the latter round. One last appearance in Formula 1 materialized in 1964 when British entrant Rob Walker entrusted Sharp with a Brabham BT11 at Watkins Glen and in Mexico, again without achieving a meaningful result.

LLOYD RUBY

As one who drove anything and everything he could get his hands on, Lloyd Ruby was a stand-out who confounded those who thought Indycar drivers would be lost if they had to turn right as well as left. From 1960 to 1977, Ruby competed in 18 consecutive Indy 500 races, leading on five occasions and achieving his best result in 1964 when he finished third. A long string of performances at the Brickyard which led to the title of his biography authored by Ted Buss: "Lloyd Ruby: The Greatest Driver Never to Win the Indy 500". However, he also collected several major victories in endurance racing driving for Ford, successfully partnering Ken Miles as the pair, who bonded like brothers when then drove together, won the prestigious 24 Hours of Daytona and the 12 Hours of Sebring events in 1966. In 1961, the Texan took a stab at Formula 1, driving a privately-entered Lotus Climax at the US Grand Prix at Watkins Glen. That single Grand Prix opportunity ended with a retirement unfortunately. Held in high esteem by his colleagues, his dignified and quiet manners were somewhat out of context of what one would expect of a racing driver. "He was a soft-spoken Texas lead foot with enormous talent," believed Dan Gurney. "He was a potential winner every time he got behind the wheel. A great oval racer who was also a great road racer."

"THOSE WERE FUN DAYS," PENSKE REMEMBERED, "ALTHOUGH I WAS WAY OVER MY HEAD."

ROGER PENSKE

Roger Penske's incredible legacy as a team owner is matched only by his outstanding success as a business entrepreneur. A walking conglomerate, with interests in hundreds of automotive-related companies, his heart and soul still remain firmly entrenched in racing. Almost every other Sunday, the "Captain" can be found on the pit wall of an American race track somewhere, surveying his team and drivers, devising race strategies and getting the job of winning done. Since its creation in the mid-'60s, Penske Racing has celebrated victories and championship titles in Indycar - with 15 victories in the Indy 500, Nascar, Can-Am, Trans-Am, the American Le Mans Series, and Formula 1. But before that outstanding track record was established, Roger Penske was simply a driver in search of success. Growing up in Cleveland, he became mad about cars early on and started to race a Corvette in SCCA events while still in college. Gradually, he became a force to be reckoned with, winning an SCCA title in 1961. Penske's first encounter with Formula 1 happened that year when he entered the US Grand Prix at Watkins Glen (along with seven other American drivers) in a year-old Cooper. A respectable eighth place spot on the grid was followed by a run to twelfth, but Penske was back in action at the Glen in 1962, this time driving a Dupont Team Zerex Lotus Climax which he very competently raced to a ninth place finish. "Those were fun days," Penske remembered, "although I was way over my head. I remember pulling out of the pits at Watkins Glen and turning a little bit too tight, bumping into the wheel of Graham Hill's BRM, with him and team owner Louis Stanley standing right there. I about had a heart attack." Fortunately, Roger Penske's business acumen and flair were already in full swing, ready to power him on to new and prosperous endeavors when he retired as a driver in 1965.

TIM MAYER

The younger brother of Teddy Mayer, Timmy grew up on the East Coast and started racing his Austin Healey when he was 21. He demonstrated early on a remarkable natural ability which encouraged him to acquire a Lotus 18 Formula Junior car in 1960. Teddy Mayer then organized a successful team in the category, running his brother and a young Peter Revson. After Timmy won the 1962 SCCA Formula Junior title, he was given a chance to race a works Cooper in the United States Grand Prix at Watkins Glen, where he retired with gearbox trouble. His ease and obvious skill behind the wheel attracted the attention of Ken Tyrrell, who viewed the American as a future bright star, but it would be Cooper who would offer the young hopeful a full season in Formula 1 as team mate to Bruce McLaren. Unfortunately, in practice for a round of the Tasman series held in New Zealand just before the start of the 1964 World Championship, Timmy Mayer crashed heavily and was killed instantly. At just 26 years old, a huge talent in the making was lost. A distraught Teddy Mayer remained in racing, co-founding McLaren Cars in 1964 and leading the team to many victories and championships after the untimely death of Bruce McLaren in 1970.

LEFT: Roger Penske running his Lotus-Climax in a non-championship Formula 1 round in Mexico in 1962. BELOW: Sitting in his Cooper-Climax, Timmy Mayer consults with Tyler Alexander before the start of the Australian Grand Prix in 1964.

TONY SETTEMBER

Southern Californian Tony Settember raced Mercedes 300SLs and Corvettes before his racing ambitions - and funding from wealthy friend Hugh Powell - took him to Europe and the exciting world of Grand Prix Racing in 1962. Unfortunately, the American's efforts were fraught with disappointment and frustration, although he did manage to see the checkered flag at his first championship outing at Aintree, where his Emeryson finished 11th. The British constructed machine was modified the following year to accept a V-8 BRM power plant, and duly renamed Scirocco. Settember's results failed to improve however in the four Grands Prix he entered, while a non-championship sortie at the Austrian Grand Prix offered some meager consolation when he finished second in a race of attrition.

PETE LOVELY

Montana native Pete Lovely was the epitome of the private Formula 1 driver. His career as a driver and entrant spanned fifty years, and included SCCA sports car wins, seven Grands Prix starts and contemporary participation in many vintage race meetings. Lovely won the very first race organized at Laguna Seca in 1957 driving a Ferrari Testarossa, eventually enjoying drives in a number of great sports cars, including a Porsche 550 Spyder, Ferraris and Corvettes. He impressive record was such that he was invited to join Team Lotus for the 1959 Monaco Grand Prix where his inexperience of open-wheel racing and the twisty street course obstructed his qualifying. His first Formula 1 start came a year later at Riverside where he quite daringly stuffed a Ferrari 625LM engine in the back of a Cooper, powering the genuine machine to eleventh place in the 1960 US Grand Prix. It would be ten years before Lovely would revisit Formula 1. In 1969, he acquired from Colin Chapman an ex-Jim Clark Lotus 49 - the very one with which Clark scored the Ford Cosworth DFV engine's debut win at Zandvoort in 1967. Lovely's first stint at the wheel of the 49 was at the Canadian Grand Prix at Mosport which brought an encouraging seventh place finish. The following season, the self-financed and adventurous privateer transported the car around Europe on the back of a VW Flatbed. Not surprisingly, Lovely failed to qualify more often than not. He did make the British Grand Prix grid at Brands Hatch though, but was not classified after running an insufficient number of laps. His last two brave attempts at Formula 1 were at the 1971 Canadian and American end-of-season races. He was not classified in both. Decades later, as a consistent entrant at the Monterey Historics, the man remembered for his passion and kindness was always more than happy to roll out the old Lotus 49, driving the precious machine in earnest, just as he did back in the good old days.

ABOVE: Privateer Formula 1 driver Pete Lovely ran the end-of-season 1969 races with his ex-works Lotus 49.

THE ADVENTUROUS LOVELY TRANSPORTED HIS LOTUS AROUND EUROPE ON THE BACK OF A VW FLATBED.

SKIP BARBER

A familiar figure in American motor racing, known especially for his famous racing schools, Skip Barber won several national SCCA championships in the mid-1960s before clinching two consecutive national titles in Formula Ford. In 1971, he purchased a March 711 with the intention of entering the Formula 1 car under the Gene Mason banner in several Grands Prix before taking it back to the US. A non-qualifier at Monaco, he finished the Dutch Grand Prix at Zandvoort but too far back to be classified. He wasn't any luckier at Mosport while he came home a distant 16th at Watkins Glen. He persevered with the March in the 1972 North American races, but to no avail. He then turned his sights to GT cars before establishing in 1975 the Skip Barber Racing School which continues to thrive today with a dozen locations across the country.

SAM POSEY

When one in the realm of motorsports evokes Sam Posey's versatility, they naturally refer to his incredible omnipresence at US tracks during his career and his ensuing success in the country's most popular categories of racing. From Trans-Am to Can-Am, to Formula 5000 and sports-prototype machines, Sam mastered them all with ease, skill and flair. But Posey's true versatility is embodied by what he has accomplished outside of racing, in the many guises his passions and gifts have produced. For three decades, Sam was as talented in the commentary box with ABC, ESPN or Speedvision as he was behind the wheel of a racing car; he's a confirmed author, writing an outstanding work on miniature trains, published in 2004; he is a qualified architect, who designed the state-of-the-art timing tower at Lime Rock in Connecticut, not to mention furniture, houses, a school and even a

firehouse; and finally, he is a fervent painter whose abstract oils have been featured in famed galleries. In hindsight, it seems only logical that someone blending the peaceful soul of an artist with the raging heart of a racing driver would one day end up in a Formula 1 car. In 1971, Posey was racing a Surtees-Chevrolet in Formula 5000 with great success when he lobbied former World Champion John Surtees for a drive in the US Grand Prix at Watkins Glen. Surtees agreed, but only after a shootout took place in practice between Posey and Dutch driver Gijs Van Lennepp. Sam

LEFT: Before devoting himself to instructing high-performance driving, Skip Barber raced in a handful of Grands Prix. Here, he puts his trusty Gene Mason Racing March 711 through its paces at Zandvoort in 1971.

delivered the goods but didn't get too far in that race unfortunately, retiring when the Cosworth expired after 15 laps. A year later, Posey was back in the seat of a works Surtees TS14, this time without having to fend off someone else's ambitions. In qualifying he was actually faster than the boss, "Big John" himself, and put in a good drive to the checkered flag, coming home 12th out of 18 finishers. "Getting to drive in a Grand Prix meant more to me than anything," Sam remembers. "Formula 1 was what I had fallen in love with when I was a kid, those guys were my heroes. It was a real highlight of my life." Today, Sam Posey is still more than ever a man of many interests, in spite of his existence having endured a difficult transition eighteen years ago when he was diagnosed with Parkinson's disease. "It's a hell of an inconvenience," Posey recently said in an interview with Charlie Rose. "I can't do buttons or change light bulbs, but driving and painting have been a saving grace for me. All the symptoms just vanish when I'm around my racing car." Sam Posey, Renaissance Man extraordinaire.

BRETT LUNGER

In many ways, Brett Lunger was one of the very last of the traditional-style Formula 1 privateers. He was part of a rare breed of American drivers who raced fulltime in Formula 1. But above all, Lunger was made of the right stuff, and a man who displayed bravery and courage in two distinctive chapters of his life, and incredible charity in a third installment, the current one. A heir to the wealthy industrial dynasty I.E. du Pont de Nemours, Brett's early racing aspirations were interrupted in 1968 when he spent 13 months as a US Marine captain in Vietnam, operating on the front line and even behind the enemy lines. Upon his safe return home he resumed his racing activities driving big-bore Can-Am and Formula 5000 machines. Enjoying some success, Lunger went to Europe and raced in Formula 2 before making his debut in Grand Prix racing in 1975 as James Hunt's team mate at Hesketh Racing. Despite his family's wealth, the young American still required outside sponsorship to secure that drive for the last three races of the '75 season. "A lot of people didn't understand that at the time, I did not have access to money," Brett explained. "Yes, the family had money, but I had not discovered leverage, or borrowing - thankfully!" In 1976, he arranged a deal with Team Surtees to race alongside future World Champion Alan Jones, delivering his best result, a tenth place finish, in Austria. The American driver's defining moment that year however, and perhaps the defining moment of his entire career, was when he helped rescue Niki Lauda from the flaming remains of his Ferrari after the Austrian's horrendous accident at the Nürburgring. In an instantaneous action, without a thought for his own safety, Lunger jumped atop the burning wreck, straddled the cockpit and hauled the World Champion out and away from peril. Six weeks later, after a miraculous recovery, Lauda was back in action at Monza where Lunger was presented by the Scuderia's Sporting Director, Daniele Audetto, with a special trophy in gratitude for his outstanding bravery. In 1977, Lunger took his Chesterfield sponsorship to Bob Sparshott's BS Fabrications team which fielded ex-works McLarens as the team contested 17 races in the following two seasons, with limited impact unfortunately. Lunger's personal best was registered at the Belgium Grand Prix at Zolder in 1978 where he finished seventh. His perseverance in Formula 1 was commendable although results were undoubtedly capped from the outset by the team's independent status and the confines of his own ability. He called time on his Grand Prix adventures at the end of the '78 season. Today, Brett Lunger devotes many long hours, along with his wife Caroline, to flying, as volunteers for the Angel Flight network, a non-profit organization which provides free air transportation to patients in need of critical care away from home. Brett Lunger: once a hero, always a hero !

WITHOUT A THOUGHT FOR HIS OWN SAFETY, LUNGER STRADDLED THE BURNING WRECK AND HAULED LAUDA OUT AND AWAY FROM PERIL.

DANNY ONGAIS

Motor racing didn't have too many drivers hailing from the paradise islands of Hawaii, but Danny Ongais was one of them, and a charger he was, often referred to as Danny "On-the-Gas". Shy and reserved outside of a racing car, he let it all out behind the wheel, his "all or nothing" approach endearing him to the crowds but also depriving his results of basic consistency. Ongais' path to Formula 1 was definitely untypical: he first started racing motorcycles in Hawaii before turning his attention to drag racing in the sixties, with a great amount of success, and then taking to SCCA road racing in the mid-1970s. Entrepreneur Ted Field, boss of the Interscope company, noted his skills and recruited Danny to drive for him in Formula 5000 in 1975, kick starting his single-seater career at the rather late age of 33. Two years later, with mentor Field now setting his sights on Formula 1, Ongais was entered in the North-American Grands Prix driving a Penske PC4. He retired early at Watkins Glen but finished a fine seventh at Mosport. Danny Ongais further acquainted himself with Formula 1 early in 1978, running in Argentina and Brazil with Mo Nunn's Ensign team, and failing to finish on both occasions. Ted Field acquired a more up-to-date Shadow DN9 for the Long Beach Grand Prix but his Hawaiian hotshoe could not come to grips with the car or the track as he failed to make the cut in pre-qualifying. A similar fate awaited Ongais a few months later at Zandvoort, marking an end to his adventures in Formula 1.

LEFT: Brett Lunger was Formula 1's last true privateer racer, running in 34 Grands Prix from 1975 to 1978. ABOVE: At the Paul Ricard circuit in Southern France, Danny Ongais ponders his F1 future in 1977.

BOBBY RAHAL

As one of American motor racing's most popular figures, Bobby Rahal needs no introduction. His stellar career as a driver spanned over two decades, most of it spent in Indycar racing where he gathered no less than 24 victories, including the 1986 Indy 500, and three Champ Car titles. Rahal's father, Mike, was an accomplished racer as well who providing his son early on with his first taste of racing. After cutting his teeth in SCCA sports car events in the early 1970s, Bobby started racing single-seaters, eventually competing in Formula Atlantic in 1977, and finishing second in the series to Canadian ace Gilles Villeneuve. Formula 1 had fueled Bobby's dreams from the outset, so he ventured to Europe to compete in Formula 3 with a Dallara-built Wolf chassis, funded by Canadian oil man Walter Wolf. That connection led to his Grand Prix racing debut at Watkins Glen with the team's Wolf WR-5. Considering his inexperience, his 20th spot on the grid, just 1.7 seconds behind team leader Jody Scheckter wasn't bad. Come race day, he put in a consistent drive to 12th. A week later, at the Canadian Grand Prix at Montreal, Rahal was amongst the fastest drivers on the track during one of the first practice sessions held on a very wet course. Pressing on, he overcooked it however and put the Wolf into the catch fencing. Unable to repair the damaged machine, the team recovered an old 1977 WR-1 from a nearby showroom, installed an engine, and Rahal duly qualified 20th! In the race, he put his head down and raced up the order, reaching 11th position after just a nine laps before his progress was hampered by a misfire which ultimately led to the demise of the Wolf's Cosworth engine. Rahal's sturdy performance induced the prospect of a full-time drive with the team in 1979, but when James Hunt was signed to replace Ferrari-bound Scheckter, he wanted all attention focused on a his single car, a demand which dashed Rahal's hopes, ultimately ending his dreams of Formula 1. The extraordinary abundance of rewards he later enjoyed in motor racing certainly pushed aside any enticement to lament over the missed opportunities of that time, as he Bobby Rahal readily admits: "Sure, I wish I would have been given a proper Formula 1 chance and the right environment, but honestly, I was successful in endurance racing, in sports cars and in Indycars, so I really can't complain." In 2000, Rahal was once again involved in Formula 1, although this time he endorsed a managerial role as CEO of Jaguar Racing with the mission of moving the British team up the Grands Prix grids. He departed from the job however, two-thirds of the way into the 2001 season, undermined by constant power struggles within the team. Bobby Rahal maintains a presence in the sport as a team owner of course, guiding Rahal-Letterman-Lanigan's efforts in Indycar, while his son, Graham, took up the mantle some time ago when he became, at 19, the youngest driver in history to win an Indycar race.

ABOVE: Bobby Rahal was entered in the North American F1 races by Walter Wolf Racing in 1978. Regrettably, he was denied other opportunities to show his unquestionable talent. RIGHT: For two consecutive seasons, Toro Rosso driver Scott Speed was offered a chance to put the United States back on the Formula 1 map. He failed to deliver however on his name's predestined promise.

FORMULA 1 FUELED BOBBY'S DREAM FROM THE OUTSET, SO HE VENTURED TO EUROPE TO COMPETE IN F3...

SCOTT SPEED

The last American driver to race in Formula 1. Scott Speed blitzed the karting world for most of his teenage years before stepping up into open-wheel racing in 2001 when he won a scholarship with the Jim Russell racing School at Sears Point. After displaying his talent in the Formula Barber Dodge and Formula Mazda championships, Speed was picked to take part in the Red Bull Driver Search contest aimed at putting a United States-born hot shoe in Formula 1. The 19-year old proved his mettle, emerging the winner and moved to Europe to race in the British Formula 3 series. It was a little too much too soon as Speed struggled, also unsettled by a rare disease called chronic ulcerative colitis which forced him to miss several races. He took a step back, rekindled his efforts and won the 2004 German and European Formula Renault championships. The following season, he finished third overall in GP2. Red Bull than offered the young hopeful a full-time seat for 2006 with its Scuderia Toro Rosso as he became the first American since Michael Andretti to enter Grand Prix racing. Speed actually enjoyed an impressive start, scoring his first point in his third race, in Australia, only to have it taken away after the stewards discovered he had overtaken another car under yellow flags. Speed did well enough to earn himself a second season with the junior Red Bull squad, but 2007 was largely disappointing, ending prematurely with a mutual parting of the ways for team and driver. A man of character who speaks his mind, Scott Speed currently races in the NASCAR Sprint Cup series, still proving that one should look beyond the catchy name.

HONDA
HONDA
HondaRacingF1.com
NTN
ENEOS

TEST DRIVERS

SO NEAR, YET SO FAR...

n the past, several American drivers tested the waters of Formula 1, while the country's future talent waits in wings for an opportunity to shine.

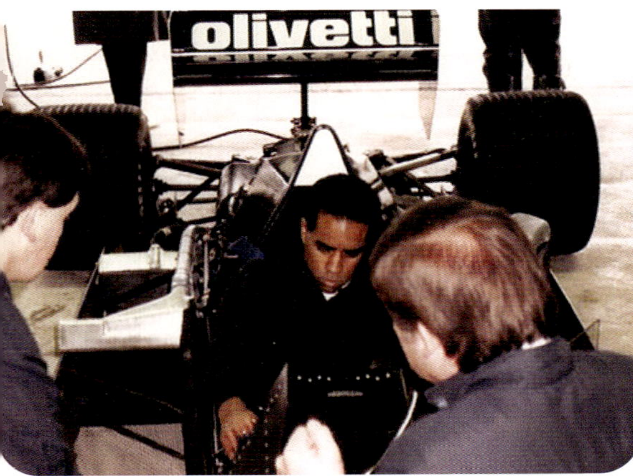

In 1979, Kevin Cogan enjoyed a run in a McLaren in a private test session in France (along with future star Alain Prost) before failing to qualify a Tyrrell in Montreal in 1980, and a private Williams at Long Beach in '81. Brabham owner Bernie Ecclestone had the American market in mind when he installed Rick Mears, and later Willy T. Ribbs in one of his cars, although neither effort resulted in an productive outcome for the drivers involved. While Michael Andretti was recruited to race for McLaren in 1993, another famous racing name was awarded a F1 test in the early 1990s: Al Unser Jr. actually put in some quite competitive times when he lapped Estoril in a Williams, but eventually declined the offer to move to F1. Fifteen years after his father, Marco Andretti

FAR LEFT: Honda granted Marco Andretti a test at Jerez in 2007. ABOVE: Conor Daly's sights are firmly set on F1.

ABOVE and RIGHT: As Caterham F1 Team's reserve driver, Alexander Rossi took part in an official F1 practice session in Spain in 2012. No one would be happier than Mario to see the young American graduate permanently to the big time. BELOW: IndyCar front-runner JR Hildebrand sampled F1 at Jerez in 2009.

got a taste of Grand Prix power when he tested a Honda at Jerez in 2007. He acquitted himself well but decided to remain within the family's Indycar circle. More recently, following Scott Speed's departure from the ranks of F1, young J.R. Hildebrand had a chance to lap Jerez in 2009 with Force India's machine. And finally, Alexander Rossi first got acquainted with F1 and BMW Sauber as a prize for winning the North American Formula BMW junior series. His subsequent seasons in Europe, racing in Formula Renault 3.5 and GP2 with Caterham, earned him a reserve role with the F1 team. Looking to the future, Conor Daly, the son of former Grand Prix driver Derek Daly, was called upon last summer by Force India to conduct some straight-line testing with the team's F1 charger. The experience naturally left him hoping for more...

Air Asia
RENAULT
SIBUR

FLYING THE AMERICAN FLAG

SCARAB | EAGLE | SHADOW | PARNELLI | PENSKE | FORCE | NART

SHELL
X-100
MOTOR OIL
Supershell
avec
SHELL
X-100
MOTOR OIL
Bitter
48

SCARAB

1960

Taking on the most prestigious and technologically advanced form of motorsports has always been a challenge for any team, regardless of its country of origin or the proficiency of its members. Overall, it's been a rocky road for American teams in Formula 1, with a variety of efforts and an even more diverse set of results.

When the Scarab Formula 1 cars of young heir Lance Reventlow showed up at Monaco in 1960, it was the culmination of an ambitious program which started two years earlier and the first true effort of an American team in post-war Grand Prix racing. Scarab had enjoyed a very successful 1958 season in sports car racing in the United States, outclassing many established manufacturers like Ferrari and Maserati. Seeking a new challenge and the realization of a personal ambition, Reventlow targeted an entry into Formula 1 in 1959, but inevitable delays pushed out the completion of Scarab's front-engine contender by almost a year. The machine's conception was entrusted to 23-year old Marshall Whitfield who had never designed a car before. He penned a conventional steel space frame chassis with double wishbone suspension and coils on all four corners. Leo Goossen from Offenshauser supplied the power of a four-cylinder 2.5 litre engine with an output of 280 bhp, supposedly matching the best European power plants of Ferrari and BRM. Practically, it only delivered a paltry 230 bhp. Unfortunately, while Reventlow had ample funding for the project, his insistence on relying completely on American components coupled with the car's outdated concept proved to be a foundation for failure. Formula 1 was on the verge of a major revolution in 1960 with the advent of the mid-engine single seater. The Scarab, in spite of its immaculate preparation, was simply a new car from a bygone era. Lance Reventlow and Chuck Daigh endured a humiliating - and dangerous - few races before the plug was pulled on the entire project.

LEFT: A new car from a bygone era, Reventlow's Scarab was simply no match for Formula 1's radical front-engine machines in 1960. ABOVE: At Monaco, Stirling Moss accepted to gauge the Scarab's performance in practice. Moss' feedback did nothing to appease Reventlow's worries.

ABOVE: The only son of Woolworth heiress Barbara Hutton, Lance Reventlow became interested in racing when he was 19. The fact that he used his personal wealth to build his own team took nothing away from the genuine talent he displayed behind the wheel.

EAGLE

1966 - 1968

The next team to step up to the plate was Dan Gurney's All American Racers in 1966. Among the great driver's partners were Carroll Shelby and the Goodyear tire company, which funded the Formula 1 arm of an operation committed first and foremost to breaking rival Firestone's hegemony at Indianapolis. The team's Grand Prix racer, the Eagle Mark 1 designed by Len Terry, was striking: clothed in dark blue, the sleek racer sported a beak-shaped nose which clearly resembled the bird of prey the machine was named after. In an effort to reduce weight, Terry developed a second iteration of the Eagle for 1967 which used metals such as magnesium and titanium. The car's four-cylinder Coventry Climax bloc was replaced by the planned V12 engine built by Weslake Research and Development of England. Car and driver's day of glory came at Spa in June of 1967. Reliability issues plagued the early part of the '68 season but on the other side of the Atlantic, Eagles were flying, with Bobby Unser scoring AAR's first victory at Indianapolis in May. By this time, Goodyear had already decided, on Carroll Shelby's advice, that its interests would be better served by focusing entirely on its USAC campaign, a decision which signaled the end of Dan Gurney's all American trials in Grand Prix racing.

LEFT: Dan Gurney and the diminutive Richie Ginther talk shop in the Monaco paddock in 1967.

Parque de Atracciones
GOODYEAR
Shell
20

SHADOW

1973 - 1980

Four years later, in 1972, Don Nichols' Shadow team joined the Formula 1 trail. Nichols was a former military intelligence officer who had established a company in California called Advanced Vehicle Systems in 1968. The company was later renamed "Shadow", perhaps a subtle reference to the founder's mysterious past. The manufacturer tackled the Can-Am series in 1970 with a radical low-line concept car driven by George Follmer, before setting up shop in England in 1972 and expanding into Formula 1, supported by the Universal Oil Products company. Ex-BRM designer Tony Southgate was commissioned to design the team's first Formula 1 car, the Shadow DN1 which featured a conventional aluminum monocoque and coke-bottle shape. Follmer and Jackie Oliver handled driving duties in 1973 before Nichols contracted Peter Revson and Frenchman Jean-Pierre Jarier to race the team's more advanced DN3 in 1974. Revson's death in South Africa was a big blow to Shadow. Jarier offered the team solace when he scored a podium finish at Monaco. British hopeful Tom Pryce was brought on board as a promising replacement, and paid back the trust bestowed upon him by winning the 1975 Race of Champions driving Southgate's latest DN5 design.

At the start of the '76 season, team sponsor UOP caught Nicols by surprise when it announced it was pulling out of Formula 1. Despite a reduced budget, Shadow fielded the new DN8 at the start of 1977 but it all went terribly wrong again at Kyalami, in South Africa. Pryce was killed when he hit a fire marshal running across the track to put out a small fire onboard team mate Reno Zorzi's car. The sore-stricken team regrouped to the best of its ability given the circumstances, hiring Alan Jones and Riccardo Patrese. In Austria, Jones put in a great performance and lifted the team's spirits when he brought Shadow a much needed Grand Prix victory. Unfortunately, a few months later, several key personnel – among them Oliver, Southgate and Patrese – left Shadow to form the new Arrows team. Clay Regazzoni and Hans Stuck raced a DN9 chassis in 1978 but without working any miracles for Nichols' now under-funded team. The following season, there was predictably no improvement as young pay-drivers Elio de Angelis and Jan Lammers learned the ropes of Formula 1. Shadow's fortunes declined miserably in 1980, to the point where its remains were sold to Theodore Racing's Teddy Yip in 1981.

ABOVE: George Follmer, Don Nichols, Alan Rees, Tony Southgate and Jackie Oliver were Shadow's core members in 1973. LEFT: Shadow's only Grand Prix victory came in Austria in 1977, courtesy of Australian Alan Jones.

TEAM
USA
Mario Andretti

PARNELLI

1975 - 1976

Backing up to 1974, the closing rounds of the season, held at Mosport and Watkins Glen, welcomed the presence of two new American Formula 1 teams: Vel's Parnelli and Penske. Both squads were warming up in preparation for a full World Championship effort the next year. Former driver Parnelli Jones and his business partner Velco Miletich had been dominant as team owners in USAC, with back to back wins at the Indy 500 in 1970 and 1971. In 1974, they commissioned British engineer Maurice Philippe to design a Formula 1 contender to be raced by Mario Andretti, with Firestone on board as a major backer. Unfortunately, the tire manufacturer decided to withdraw from racing in 1975, leaving the team holding the bag right in the middle of a season marked by mechanical failures of various types. With insufficient funding to ensure the car's proper development, Parnelli ran two more races in 1976 before its Formula 1 operation was shelved.

LEFT: Mario Andretti's abundant talent and dedication were simply not enough to elevate the under-funded Parnelli team's level of performance in 1975. When sponsor Firestone withdrew from racing at the end of the season, the writing was on the wall for the American squad.

PENSKE

1974 - 1976

Given Penske Racing's outstanding success in the '70s in so many forms of US racing, Roger Penske's decision to venture into Formula 1 in 1974 appeared quite rational. It was an important step on several levels however, as it represented the team's first experience in designing and building its own car. Penske headquartered its Grand Prix operation in Poole, England where former Brabham draughtsman Geoff Ferris designed the wholly conventional Penske PC1. In typical Penske style, the immaculate First National City machine was meticulously built and prepared for Mark Donohue's debut in the 1974 North American races. In 1975, following a string of disappointing results, the PC1 was replaced with a March customer chassis. Donohue's performances immediately improved until tragedy struck in Austria, when the American died from a brain hemorrhage sustained after a massive crash in the warm-up practice session. The misfortune dealt a huge blow to the American team and to Roger Penske himself, who lost not only his principal driver, but a close friend. Gathering all its strengths, the crew put its head down and persevered, fielding a brand new Penske PC3 for John Watson in 1976. Despite the British driver's best efforts, the team still remained a mid-field runner, until Ferris designed the much improved PC4 chassis. Armed with the new mount, Watson put himself on the podium in France and later that summer, upon the team's difficult return to Zeltweg in Austria, both team and driver claimed a highly emotional first Grand Prix win, exactly one year after Mark Donohue's death. At the end of the '76 season, Roger Penske pondered his two years of struggles, tragedy and single victory; his team had undoubtedly given Formula 1 its best shot, but the price of such hardship had simply been too high. Consequently, Penske retreated from Grand Prix racing.

LEFT and ABOVE: Even in the highly capable hands of Mark Donohue, the wholly conventional Penske PC1 designed by Geoff Ferris was a disappointment. Several chassis later, John Watson raced the much improved Penske PC4 to an emotional victory in Austria in 1976. The Ulsterman's triumph went a long way towards healing Penske's wounds, one year after the tragic loss of Mark Donohue.

Ford
Ford
15
BP

FORCE

1985 - 1986

America's next Formula 1 exponent was another prominent figure of US motor racing. With countless wins and championships under his name, legendary team owner Carl Haas was certainly a force to be reckoned with when he entered Formula 1 in 1985. And FORCE (Formula One Race Car Engineering) was exactly the moniker of the company set up to build his Grand Prix challenger. On paper, Haas's outfit looked quite impressive: proper funding was provided by the Beatrice Foods conglomerate, an exclusive engine deal was secured with Ford, and the team's organization chart read like a who's who of Formula 1, with promising engineers Neil Oatley and Ross Brawn entrusted with design work, while former McLaren headmen Teddy Mayer and Tyler Alexander were on board overseeing race operations. Haas even convinced former World Champion Alan Jones to exit a plushy retirement and resume driving duties.

Ford's twin-turbo V6 power plant was late in development, so the team's Beatrice-Lola THL1 made its debut at Monza in the summer of '85 with the straight-four Hart engine. It's worth noting that Lola Cars, for which Haas acted as its American agent, actually had nothing to do with the car's design or development; the manufacturer's name was used just to add credibility to the operation. Way off the pace in its early races, the elegant red and blue machine was finally fitted in 1986 with its prescribed Ford-badged Cosworth engine, while a second car was fielded for French driver Patrick Tambay. The team also recruited a young designer by the name of Adrian Newey, who would later conceive a plethora of winning Formula 1 cars for Williams, McLaren and, more recently, Red Bull. There was marked improvement for the team and its drivers in the latter part of the season, with Jones and Tambay scoring a few championship points. Unfortunately, a change of management at Beatrice Foods left Carl Haas without a sponsor for 1987. Attempts to find new backers were unsuccessful and left the cigar-touting manager with little option but to wind up its Formula 1 operation. Assuredly, the divide between the team's potential, given all the right ingredients it appeared to enjoy from the outset, and its meager results was huge. It proved once again that while resources were paramount, one still required the 'X' factor to succeed in Formula 1.

LEFT and ABOVE: To mount an attack on Formula 1 in 1976, Carl Haas put together an impressive line-up which included former McLaren headman Teddy Mayer and 1980 World Champion Alan Jones. The American team still failed to make a lasting impression.

FERRARI NART

1964

There is no denying Luigi Chinetti's contribution to Ferrari's legendary history. As an ambitious visionary, he established the manufacturer's presence in the United States, and built its prestigious reputation in the world's most critical and richest market. As a discerning and successful judge of talent, he led many drivers to the gates of Maranello, boosting the careers of American F1 drivers Phil Hill, Dan Gurney and Richie Ginther.

Once a talented driver, Chinetti triumphed at Le Mans in 1932 and 1934, driving an Alfa Romeo. On the eve of Italy's entrance into the Second World War, he migrated to America and became a US citizen, retaining a fervent link with his home country through his close relationship with Enzo Ferrari. In 1949, he again won at Le Mans, partnered in one of Ferrari's 166 Barchetta's for the constructor's first visit to the Sarthe circuit, but driving nearly 23 hours himself.

In 1951, Luigi Chinetti founded the North American Racing Team, Ferrari's most consistently successful privateer team. Under its banner, he installed the Rodriguez brothers - Ricardo and Pedro - in scarlet red machines and sent the Mexican duo in its way to stardom. More importantly, he made Americans directly aware of Ferrari's thriving presence in sports car racing, a perception which helped instigate the manufacturer's commercial success in the United States.

In a bizarre twist of Ferrari politics, Chinetti's NART also sealed the win of the 1964 Formula 1 World Champion John Surtees. A huge row between Enzo Ferrari and the Italian Automobile Federation over the latter's refusal to back the homologation of the manufacturer's new 250LM sports car, led Ferrari to relinquish its Italian competitor's license. The Scuderia's cars therefore appeared at Watkins in the blue and white American colors of NART. In a sense, the plot was a fitting tribute to Luigi Chinetti's long standing role as Enzo Ferrari's loyal representative, confidant and second self.

ABOVE: Luigi Chinetti's business acumen as well as his passion for Ferrari instigated the Italian company's success in the United States. LEFT: John Surtees' NART liveried Ferrari rounds the hairpin at Mexico in 1964, where Lorenzo Bandini and Pedro Rodriguez also raced under the banner of the North American Racing Team.

MADE IN USA

ENGINE | TIRES | CHASSIS | SUPER COMPUTERS | SAFETY

ENGINES

FORD DFV: 155 WINS

In the last fifty years, America's presence in Formula 1 has extended way beyond its driver or team representations, with innumerable US companies supplying their innovative engineering expertise to the highest level of international motor racing. Their successful involvement often proved decisive in sustaining Grand Prix racing's healthy continuity.

Little did anyone dream that Jimmy Clark's win in the 1967 Dutch Grand Prix would usher in a golden age for Formula 1. That day, the Scotsman powered his Lotus 49 to victory using for the very first time Ford's illustrious Cosworth DFV. It was a stunning debut in the sandy dunes of Zandvoort, and a historic one for an engine which would ultimately claim a total of 155 wins from 262 races between 1967 and 1985.

Ford's involvement originally stemmed from Lotus founder Colin Chapman's quest for a new power plant following the entrance in 1966 of regulations which raised Formula 1's maximum engine capacity from 1.5 to 3.0 litres. Chapman subsequently contacted engineer Keith Duckworth of Cosworth, who said he could produce a competitive three-litre engine, if a £100,000 (approximately $240,000 at that time) development budget could be provided. The Lotus boss raised the issue with Walter Hayes, head of public relations for Ford in the United Kingdom, who then convinced the manufacturer to commit the required resources for the development of a 3-litre V8 with twin overhead camshafts and four valves per cylinder, destined for glory as the DFV (double four valve).

Starting mid-1966, Duckworth dedicated all his time to the engine's nine month gestation, living the life of a recluse, working 16 hours a day. First dynamometer runs gave a power output of 408 bhp which met Chapman's specifications. The engine's initial track testing was performed by Cosworth partner Mike Costin driving a Lotus 49 at Hethel Aerodome, near the team's workshops. Clark's landmark triumph in Holland led to more dominant performances in Britain, the United States and Mexico. Initially, as the engine's funder, Ford had no intentions to sell the DFV to any other teams. But in the absence of any real competition, with most other Formula 1 engines underpowered, too heavy or unreliable, Walter Hayes believed Ford's interests would be best served if the unit was made available to other teams starting in 1968, with a view of potentially dominating Grand Prix racing thereafter. Demand was immediate and increased dramatically over the following months. The Ford-Cosworth DFV was first released to Ken Tyrrell's Matra team and to McLaren, but eventually, any Formula 1 team, big or small, would have access to an engine which was competitive, light, compact, easy to work with and relatively cheap, at approximately $18,000.

After Clark's tragic death at Hockenheim in early 1968, it fell to team mate Graham Hill to win the 1968 World Championship with the DFV-powered Lotus, which also took the manufacturers' crown. In 1969, every single World Championship race was won by DFV-powered machines, a feat repeated in 1973. In the end, the legendary power plant engine enjoyed an eighteen-year tenure in Formula 1. Its longevity was helped however by the arrival of ground effects in 1977, as the Cosworth's V-configuration and angled cylinders left ample space under the car for the necessary venturi and under-body profile of the fabulous wing-cars. The inception of the turbo era in the early 1980s gradually put the DFV out of contention. Even with consistent development the unit could not keep up with the power onslaught of the 1.5 liter turbocharged engines. Tyrrell driver Michele Alboreto took the Ford Cosworth engine to its last win in 1983 in Detroit.

In the late 1980s, Ford supplanted the DFV with a new engine, the HB, which won 11 races between 1989 and 1993, before it was replaced by the Zetec V8 F1 which powered Michael Schumacher to his first World Championship title for Benetton in 1994. In 1997, Cosworth, then owned by Ford, entered into a three-year partnership with Stewart Grand Prix, eventually buying the Formula 1 outfit and supplying engines to the rechristened Jaguar squad, alongside several other customer teams. After its long and fruitful involvement in Grand Prix racing, Ford departed Formula 1 in 2004.

LEFT: Ford's glorious DFV was Formula 1's most successful engine, with a remarkable 155 Grands Prix wins. ABOVE: A Chrysler financed Lamborghini engine enjoyed a three-year presence in Formula1, powering the French Larousse team. Contrary to Ford, the American manufacturer never put its full backing behind the venture.

GOODYEAR
EAGLE

TIRES

GOODYEAR 368 WINS

Tires have always played a crucial role in the history of Formula 1, undergoing massive evolution over the decades, with different manufacturers and specifications used throughout. When Goodyear scored its first victory in 1965 at the Mexican Grand Prix, there was no stopping the American manufacturer who reaped an additional 367 Grand Prix wins until its withdrawal from the sport in 1998. Firestone also enjoyed an impressive period of success, between 1969 and 1972, supplying winning rubber to the Ferrari team as well as to World Champions Graham Hill, Jochen Rindt and Emerson Fittipaldi. The manufacturer ceased its involvement in 1974.

Tire technology in Formula 1 really took off with the advent of slick tires, first used at the Spanish Grand Prix in 1971. When Michelin entered the fray in 1977 with its innovative radial tire, a battle royal between Goodyear and the French company dramatically accelerated compound development. Viewed by many as an art which borders on alchemy, or even "black magic", tire manufacturing followed the exponential performance increase provided by ground effects and turbo engines in Formula 1 in the early 1980s. During qualifying sessions, front-running teams were offered super soft tires which lasted only a handful of laps, the duration of a driver's "banzaï" run to pole position.

In between races, Goodyear engineers would spare no expense to try to define the optimum tire for a specific track, often enduring countless hours of testing with their contracted drivers grinding around, sifting through dozens of compounds in search for the day's holy rubber. The American manufacturer from Akron, Ohio, introduced its own radial slick tire in 1984, while Michelin left Formula 1 a year later. It also initiated at this time the use of tire heating blankets, a pre-heater system which brought compounds up to optimal temperatures before a car took to a track. With Pirelli as its only rival on the tire front, Goodyear found itself in a position of near-total dominance, the Italian company winning just three races between 1985 and 1991, when it also left Formula 1. Finally, Bridgestone arrived to end Goodyear's monopoly in 1997, but at the end of that year, the FIA banned slicks, imposing the use of grooved tires in an effort to reduce cornering speeds. Uninterested in pursuing what it saw as a technological dead-end, Goodyear brought to a close 33 years of uninterrupted participation in Grand Prix racing.

LEFT: Goodyear's multi-decade tenure in Formula1 was rewarded with 367 Grand Prix wins and a huge benefit in terms of tire development. BELOW: In the early 1970s, Firestone was Lotus' partner of choice.

MP4/1

CHASSIS

CARBON FIBER

After ground effects and turbocharged engines took hold of Formula 1, chassis development received its own striking technological advancement in 1981. When McLaren unveiled its first carbon-composite MP4/1, the winds of change started blowing through the entire sport. Traditionally, Formula 1 conception had relied on flat aluminum panels fixed together to form a chassis' monocoque. But McLaren engineer John Barnard, who had designed the 1980 Indy 500 winning Chaparral 2K, had a revolutionary belief that a highly rigid tub structure could be achieved with the use of carbon fiber, a material which had been used in small parts by Formula 1 since the mid-70s, but never for a full chassis construction. To turn his ground-breaking idea into reality, the adventurous Barnard worked with the experimental department of an American aerospace company called Hercules, located in Utah. The end result was a chassis constructed from just five major composite mouldings (where up to 50 sections of aluminum had been required previously), which was incredibly light and even more rigid than Barnard had imagined. McLaren driver John Watson remembers his first track test of the radical design: "It was like flying in the Concorde when you've only ever flown in a 747." Hercules' expertise and craftsmanship, as well as Barnard's pioneering idea of course, were rewarded at the British Grand Prix at Silverstone in the summer of 1981, when Watson took the car's first win. Fellow engineers, and indeed many drivers, expressed reservations concerning carbon fiber however, pointing to the uncertainty surrounding the composite material's reaction in the event of an accident. Watson put those worries to rest a few weeks later, demonstrating the concept's bullet-proof strength when he emerged unscathed from a massive 140 mph impact at Monza's daunting Lesmo corner. Born out of the incredible vision of John Barnard and Hercules' command of composite technology, the McLaren MP4/1 blazed the trail for a whole new generation of safer Formula 1 cars.

LEFT and ABOVE: The idea of a carbon fiber chassis was the brainchild of creative McLaren engineer John Barnard. Helped by Hercules' expertise, the concept completely revolutionized Formula 1 chassis design.

BMW Sauber F1 Team
Albert3.
intel
DALCO
ANSYS
FLUENT

SUPER COMPUTERS THE INTEL INSIDE

In the 1990s, aerodynamics became the most important factor in Formula 1 car design. It was nearly the only performance enhancing area of interest, as only very marginal gains - limited by stringent regulations - could be obtained from engine or other mechanic component development. Grand Prix racing's commercial success during this period boosted team budgets considerably, and with this increase in resources came heavy investments into aerodynamic studies conducted in wind tunnels.

Computer aided design (CAD) quickly replaced drawing boards, allowing engineers to work a lot faster and more efficiently. Gradually, the modeling became so complex that top teams such as McLaren, Ferrari or Williams employed dozens of people entirely devoted to the design of aero bits and their validation in full-scale wind tunnels working almost 24 hours a day. It was the advent of Computational Fluid Dynamics, or CFD, the analysis of an object, in this case a Formula 1 car, within a computer simulation, using basic laws of physics governing air flow. A Formula 1 team's design department evolved into a titan of technological power, mainly provided by Silicon Valley's most notable IT companies. Hewlett Packard supplied its servers to Williams for breathtaking calculations and computing far beyond the reach of human ability. Sun Microsystems, through its network of powerful desktop workstations and servers dedicated to CAD and trackside monitoring, was a key technology partner with McLaren for many years. Since 2004, the brain behind the Sauber Formula 1 team has been a supercomputer named Albert, now in its third iteration. The Intel powered processing system, weighing 21 tons and measuring roughly twenty nine and a half feet long, is one of the most powerful units in the automotive industry. AMD, based in Sunnyvale, California, a global manufacturer of high performance PC processors and flash memory devices, has been a Ferrari sponsor since 2002, also supplying the legendary Scuderia with AMD-based systems for performance diagnostics. Intel, Hewlett Packard, Sun Microsystems and AMD are part of the new frontier in automotive design, technical development, diagnostics and safety. American IT companies are Formula 1's new age wizards of winning.

LEFT: The Swiss Sauber team relies on the titanic power of its 'Albert 3' super-computer for all its design and simulator work. The system, based on Intel technology, boasts a total weight of 21 tons.
ABOVE: Microsoft Dynamics is one of many US IT companies currently involved in Formula 1.

BELL

SAFETY PROTECTION

Back in the 1950s and early '60s, in spite of the many tragedies which afflicted Grand Prix racing, safety was of no real concern in Formula 1. As unprecedented advances in technology and aerodynamics produced a remarkable increase in the cars performances, an acute awareness for protection emerged. Gradually, the sport's governing body developed and applied measures to contain the consequences - for drivers as well as for spectators - of accidents, eventually achieving levels of risk which are now minimal for all involved. At the forefront of safety in the field of protective headgear since its inception by Roy Richter in 1954, Bell Helmets rapidly earned the trust of drivers across the world. In 1968, the company introduced the first full-face helmet, the Star. Dan Gurney's immediate adoption of the revolutionary lid in 1968 prompted his Formula 1 colleagues to do the same. Over the years, the company has remained at the edge of technology, pioneering an outstanding number of innovations in all areas of modern helmetry, with its lightweight materials shells, ventilations systems, and advanced aerodynamic designs.

A current mandatory accessory to the Formula 1 drivers' helmet since 2003, the Head and Neck Support System (HANS), a carbon-fiber collar that fits around a driver's neck and restrains the head and neck in the event of a crash or collision, was developed in the 1980s by Robert Hubbard, an engineering professor at Michigan State University. Initially designed in as a protective device for powerboat racers, it has since been adopted by most motor racing categories.

Exclusive engineering and technical innovation have always been stringent guidelines followed by the manufacturers of race wear. For decades, industry leaders Hinchman and Simpson set the benchmark for craftsmanship, supplying their custom, tailor made fire resistant products - race suits, gloves, underwear - to the very best without any sense of compromise. For safety has no price.

LEFT: In 1968, Dan Gurney became the first Formula 1 driver to wear Bell's innovative full face helmet.
RIGHT: The HANS device is now a safety item compulsory inall major motor racing series worldwide.

CYNAR

HOLLYWOOD

GOES TO THE RACES

American Pete Aron was a Grand Prix winner in 1966. At least on the big screen. Billed as "the greatest racing film ever made", John Frankenheimer's 1966 epic 'Grand Prix' truly captured the visceral thrill and glamour of Formula 1. The film amazed a wide international audience, and also contributed a hefty profit to MGM Studios' bottom line.

RIGHT: James Garner took the lead role of Pete Aron in 'Grand Prix'. BELOW: John Frankenheimer's production team prepares for a scene along the Monte Carlo harbour.

Before the release of 'Grand Prix' in 1966, Hollywood's need for speed was confined to a handful of second-rate movies which exploited motor racing's elusive qualities as a mere backdrop. From the outset, the film's director John Frankenheimer broke new ground, pulling out all the stops to capture the exhilarating and dramatic realities of Formula 1. For starters, he relied on Technicolor, stereo and Cinerama to wonder audiences. Secondly, his ascribed pursuit of authenticity led the film to dive into actual races as Frankenheimer blended footage shot at a proper Grand Prix, like Monaco and Spa, with in-car scenes shot with the actors to create a

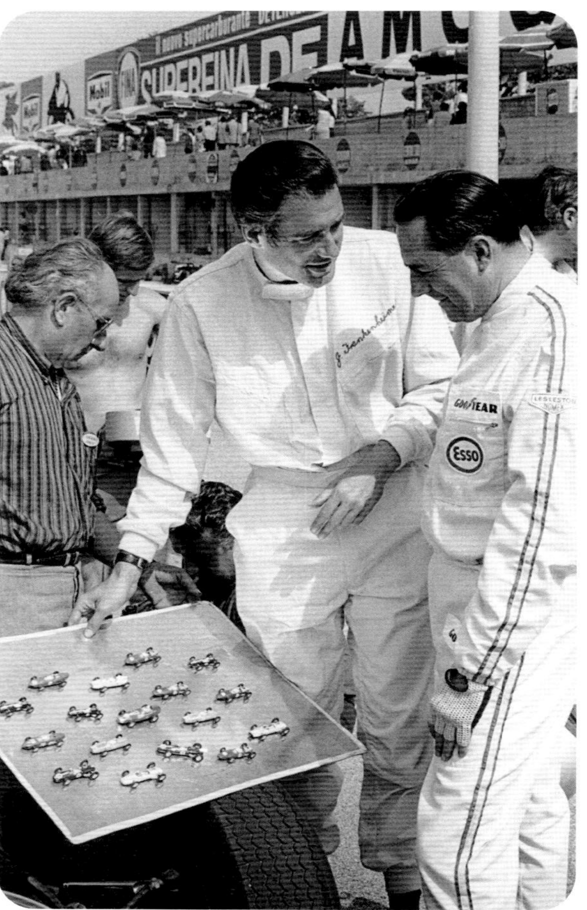

sequence. The end result was truly spectacular, especially at a time when most people followed racing via newspaper photos or radio broadcast. During pre-production, actor Steve McQueen was the studio and the director's first choice for the part of American driver Pete Aron. Given his devoted passion for motor sport, Hollywood's super star expressed genuine interest in the role. But when Frankenheimer sent his assistant Eddie Lewis in his stead to initiate contract negotiations, McQueen took and instant dislike to Lewis and backed out of the project. Instead, the role of Pete Aron went to James Garner. McQueen of course, would go on to produce his own epic - Le Mans, a few years later. Grand Prix's cast was a roster of international stars which included French idol Yves Montand, England's Brian Bedford, Italy's Antonio Sabato and American actress Eva Marie Saint. In order to accustom actors with the basics of race car driving and instill a sense of confidence behind the wheel, all endured an intense three-week training session at Jim Russell's racing school. Garner himself spent a considerable amount of time lapping the Willow Springs race track in California in various machines, under the watchful eye of Bob Bondurant. Frankenheimer understandably took a small amount of artistic license when it came to the film's cars, with Jim Russell outfitting his fleet of Formula 3 cars to resemble the thoroughbred F1 racers of the day. When things got rolling, Frankenheimer and his

LEFT: MGM Studios' first choice as lead role was Steve McQueen, seen here with Ronnie Bucknum at Monaco in 1965. MIDDLE: Jack Brabham helps Frankenheimer stage the start of a race.
ABOVE: Fangio and Garner meet on the grid at Monza, as journalist Franco Lini looks on. RIGHT: A mock-up Ferrari, complete with dummy-driver, blasts off Monza's banking in the film's dramatic final racing scene.

Esso
METTI UN
NEL MOTORE
EXTRA
BARDAHL
Reg. Parnell (Racing) Ltd.
CASTROL
VALVOLINE
CHAMPION
COUPONS
Supershell

MGM production team were a permanent fixture at the European races all throughout the 1966 season, and it all happened under the eagle-eye of renowned photographer Bernard Cahier. Hired initially as a technical consultant and for networking purposes, the Frenchman was eventually offered a role as a prominent photo journalist when shooting began in Monaco, much to his delight. "John had me all dressed up , with a mustache and little hat," Cahier remembered. "When we went to see the rushes, I told him it looked terrible. I convinced him that he should let me play myself, with no disguise, and allow me to bring along some of my friends who were photographers and journalists. The next day, we re-shct the scenes and it looked great. That said, it was hard work, even more tiring than covering a real race, as the days were long, with a lot of time spent waiting. But we were paid well." The movie also had its skeptics, among which was Enzo Ferrari, who did not want his scarlet red machines to be any part of the project, a prospect Frankenheimer thought would crush the film's credibility. After shooting in Monte Carlo, the director put together a thirty-minute rush, traveled to Maranello and showed Ferrari a preview of things to come. Highly impressed by the quality of what he saw, and suddenly aware of the exposure his cars and name would receive, Ferrari gave the American director the green light. Forty-two years later, "Grand Prix" remains the ultimate cinematography celebration of Formula 1.

FAR LEFT: 'Scott Stoddard' exits the Monza paddock before the Italian Grand Prix.
LEFT: Phil Hill and actor Yves Montand at Spa.
MIDDLE: In the 1977 film 'Bobby Deerfield', Al Pacino's character was represented by Carlos Pace in the racing scenes. ABOVE: At Monaco, photographer Bernard Cahier shares a beer with actor Kirk Douglas.

RACING IN THE USA

SEBRING | RIVERSIDE | WATKINS GLEN | LONG BEACH | LAS VEGAS | DETROIT | DALLAS | PHOENIX | INDIANAPOLIS

With nine different locations, various commercial fortunes and two periods of interruption, the United States Grand Prix was a difficult business to sustain over the years. The event's history is inextricably bound to that of Formula 1 however, with many outstanding races and an abundance of defining moments.

SEBRING

Since the inception of the World Championship in 1950, the majority of Formula 1 races took place in Europe, but in early December 1959, teams and drivers ventured across the Atlantic to Florida and the inaugural United States Grand Prix. The event was held at Sebring, the home of the 12 Hours endurance sports car race, on a 5.2 mile course laid out over an old military airfield. The last race of the year resulted in a three-way battle for the title between Cooper-Climax drivers Jack Brabham and Stirling Moss, and Ferrari stalwart Tony Brooks and, with the nimble rear-engine British cars pitted against the Scuderia's chunky front-engine Dino. The field also included six American drivers, notably Roger Ward at the wheel of an under-powered Kurtis-Offenhauser midget which was way out of its league on Sebring's long straight-aways. In the end, victory fell into the hands of young Bruce McLaren, while Brabham clinched the world title, a first for the Australian as well as for a rear-engine car. Black Jack's performance eventually led Cooper to enter the low-slung machine at Indianapolis in 1961, an appearance which foreran the rear-engine revolution which would sweep the Speedway in the following five years. As for Bruce McLaren, his triumph at Sebring, at the tender age of 22 years and 104 days, made him the youngest driver ever to win a Grand Prix, a record which held until Fernando Alonso's victory in Hungary in 2003.

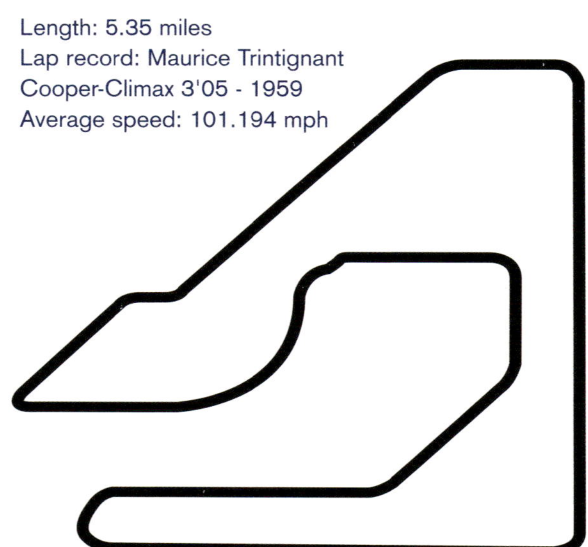

FAR RIGHT: The Cooper's of Jack Brabham and Stirling Moss blast off the grid of the very first United States Grand Prix.

RIVERSIDE

Sebring's famed promoter, Alec Ulmann, decided to head out west for the second US Grand Prix, staged at Riverside International Raceway in late November 1960, a track set near the San Bernardino Mountains just east of Los Angeles. The circuit's lack of infrastructure, a common inadequacy in those days, saw Formula 1's teams set up shop in local garages scattered around the area. A state of affairs which offered photographer Bernard Cahier an opportunity to snap a series of amusing shots of race cars running in city traffic as their drivers commuted to the race track. The final event of the season took place 10 weeks after the last European race at Monza, and Ferrari did not bother to travel to California. Phil Hill opted for a ride in a BRP Cooper however. On race day, only a small crowd of Riverside veterans were on hand to witness the victory of Stirling Moss, driving Rob Walker's Scottish blue Lotus-Climax, in front of Innes Ireland in a works Lotus and Bruce McLaren's Cooper. Jack Brabham was crowned World Champion for the second consecutive year. A young aspiring champion by the name of Jim Hall drove a good race, running fourth before dropping to seventh at the end when his transmission failed, which forced the future Chaparral genius to push his Lotus to the finish line.

LEFT: On his way to the race track, John Surtees' Lotus blends into local traffic.

Length: 3.484 miles
Lap record: Jack Brabham
Cooper-Climax 1'56''3 - 1960
Average speed: 101.383 mph

WATKINS GLEN

For whatever reasons, the previous two attempts to introduce Grand Prix racing to the American public were not met with success. But once Formula 1 settled into its regular home at Watkins Glen, loyal and appreciative fans turned out in masses at the upstate New York venue for almost twenty years. "The Glen", as it is known in the motor racing world, quickly became part of racing folklore. Every year, the laid-back 'Indian Summer' atmosphere encouraged campers to travel to the Fingers Lake region and watch the action. Spectators converged at the Kendall Technical Center to get a glimpse of teams and drivers housed within the large garage. The winding 3.4-mile course always offered its share of challenges and exciting races. Lotus driver Innes Ireland won the inaugural event in 1961 and his only World Championship race. Graham Hill was unbeatable from 1963 to 1965, while Ferrari driver John Surtees became the only man in history to be crowned World Champion on two and four wheels in 1964. Jimmy Clark's Lotus was powered to victory in 1966 by the raucous BRM H16, the only success of a 16-cylinder engine in F1. In 1970, Emerson Fittipaldi won his first Grand Prix at 23 years of age, a feat repeated by rising star François Cevert the following year. In 1973, the race should have been Jackie Stewart's 100th and last Grand Prix, but the triple-World Champion was denied the distinction when Ken Tyrrell withdrew his entries following the tragic death of Cevert in qualifying. Gradually, Formula 1 became tired of the Glen and of its outdated infrastructure, the lack of accommodations in the area and the drunken mobs of fans in the infamous Bog. In 1979, the genius of Gilles Villeneuve overcame the rain and fog all weekend to capture a resounding success for Ferrari.

ABOVE: McLaren boys Revson and Hulme lead the pack off the grid at the Glen in 1972. LEFT: Former World Champion turned commentator Jackie Stewart interviews 1974 winner Carlos Reutemann. RIGHT: Elio de Angelis' Shadow on its way to 7th in 1979.

World Champion Alan Jones was the last man to win in Formula 1 at Watkins Glen in 1980, but only after a scintillating drive from Bruno Giacomelli came to a premature halt when the electrics failed on the Italian's Alfa Romeo. Grand Prix racing left the Glen permanently thereafter.

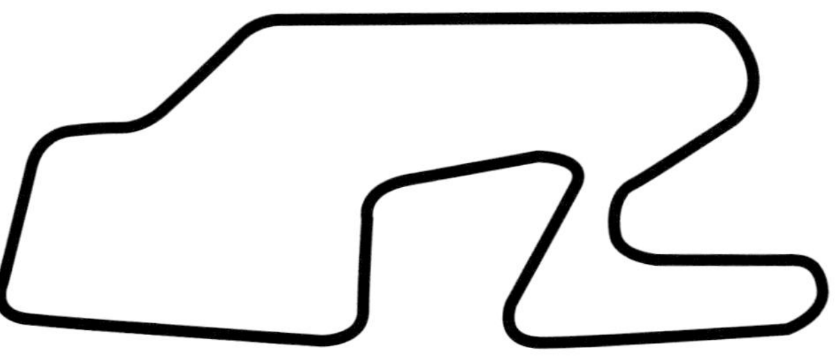

Length: 3.663 miles
Lap record: Alan Jones - Williams 1'34''068 - 1980
Average speed: 129.244 mph

18
GOODYEAR
27
ALBILAD

TOYOTA
TOYOTA
Canon
CRYSEN
BRIDGESTONE
benetton
benetton
FLY saudia
FLY saudia
FLAGGING

LONG BEACH

For five years, America enjoyed the privilege of a double-bill when it came to Formula 1, with Long Beach joining Watkins Glen on the Grand Prix calendar from 1976 to 1980. The West Coast seaside city was California's answer to Monaco, its sunny and vibrant atmosphere proving highly popular with race fans and competitors. Clay Regazzoni and Ferrari were the first to master the tricky street course. Sadly, the Swiss driver's career also came to a painful end at Long Beach in 1980 when a massive crash caused by a brake failure left him paralyzed from the waist down. Mario Andretti made history in 1977 when, driving for Lotus, he became the first American to win a United States Grand Prix. After a two year hiatus from racing, Niki Lauda produced a remarkable come-back in 1982, winning on his third outing that season at Long Beach. One year later, the Austrian was runner-up to McLaren team mate John Watson. Unfortunately, escalating organizing costs forced promoter Chris Pook to turn away from F1 at the end of 1983. The Long Beach Grand Prix has remained a permanent fixture on the motor racing agenda as part of CART and IndyCar's schedule.

LEFT: Patrick Tambay leads Keke Rosberg into the first corner of the 1983 Long Beach Grand Prix. RIGHT: Jacques Laffite's Ligier in 1976. BELOW: Watson and Lauda on the winner's podium in 1983.

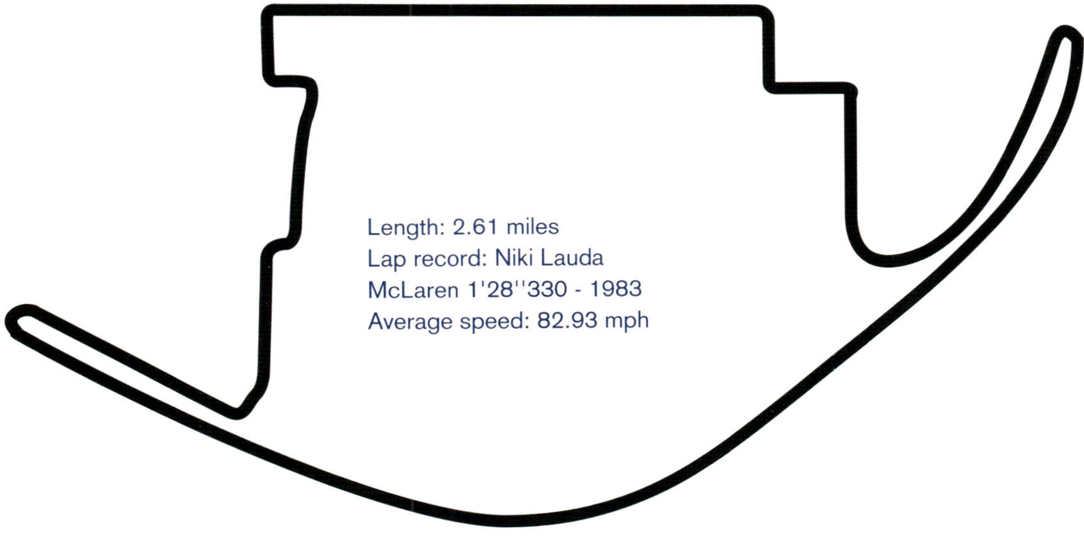

LAS VEGAS

As absurd as the idea may seem in today's era of state-of-the-art, purpose built racing facilities, Las Vegas once saw the fastest cars in the world race around a parking lot. Promoters of the gambling capital of the world had drummed up the ill-fated concept as a way of tapping into a "new market". The result was a 2.2-mile track cramped into a 75-acre lot next to the Caesars Palace Hotel, devoid of high-speed sweepers, fast straight-aways, or even the odd landmark, as there wasn't a tree, a bush or a blade of grass in sight. Fourteen corners and cement walls were Las Vegas' only claim to character. The race's first edition in 1981 was a title decider between four drivers, with Carlos Reutemann the clear favorite. But it all fell apart for the moody Argentinean on race day when he was defeated by a recalcitrant gear-box and Williams team-mate Alan Jones, while Brazilian Nelson Piquet was crowned World Champion. The following year saw another title-decider race, this time between Keke Rosberg and John Watson. The former won the jackpot while Tyrrell driver Michele Alboreto reaped his very first Grand Prix win. The race was also Mario Andretti's last drive in Formula 1, as well as Eddie Cheever's first podium, achieved at the wheel of a Ligier-Matra. Given the small attendance generated on both occasions by Vegas' motor racing publicity stint, the event disappeared, quite deservedly, from the Formula 1 calendar.

Length: 2.471 miles
Lap record: Michele Alboreto
Tyrrell 1'19''639 - 1982
Average speed: 102.523 mph

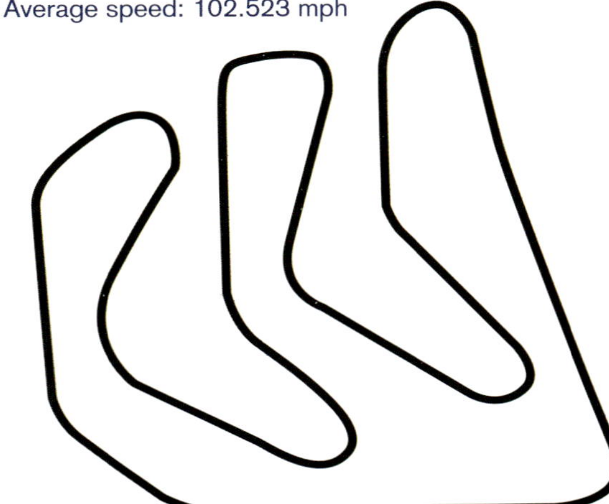

RIGHT: Prost leads Renault team-mate Arnoux at the start in 1982. BELOW LEFT: Vegas was the scene of Mario Andretti's last F1 race in 1982.
BELOW: Alan Jones conquered Sin City in 1982.

NISSAN
DATSUN
CAESARS PALACE
GRAND PRIX
CAESARS PALACE GRAND PRIX
RENAULT elf
elf
parmalat

AMM FIAMM
LOTO
26
elf

LEFT: Jacques Laffite's Ligier in 1986.
ABOVE: Shadowed by the Spirit of Detroit, Senna captured his fourth career win in Motor City in 1986.

DETROIT

In 1982, Motor City pursued the theme of street races in America, offering its impressive urban backdrop to Formula 1 for six years. Intended to revitalize Detroit's downtown area, the original tight and twisty 2.5-mile track was centered around the city's Renaissance Center, and featured 17 turns, most of which were slow, 90-degree corners. The narrow and bumpy course often threw a wrench in the works, but John Watson produced the drive of his life to win Detroit's inaugural event after launching his McLaren from 17th on the grid. In 1983, Tyrrell's Michele Alboreto scored his second Grand Prix victory and the last of a record 155 wins for the legendary Ford Cosworth DFV engine. Brazilian ace Ayrton Senna worked his magic for three consecutive years, prevailing twice with Lotus, in '86 and '87, and then with McLaren in 1988. Mitigated financial success coupled with the venue's inadequate facilities led to Formula 1's departure from Detroit in 1988.

Length: 2.879 miles
Lap record: Ayrton Senna
McLaren 1'40''464 - 1987
Average speed: 89.57 mph

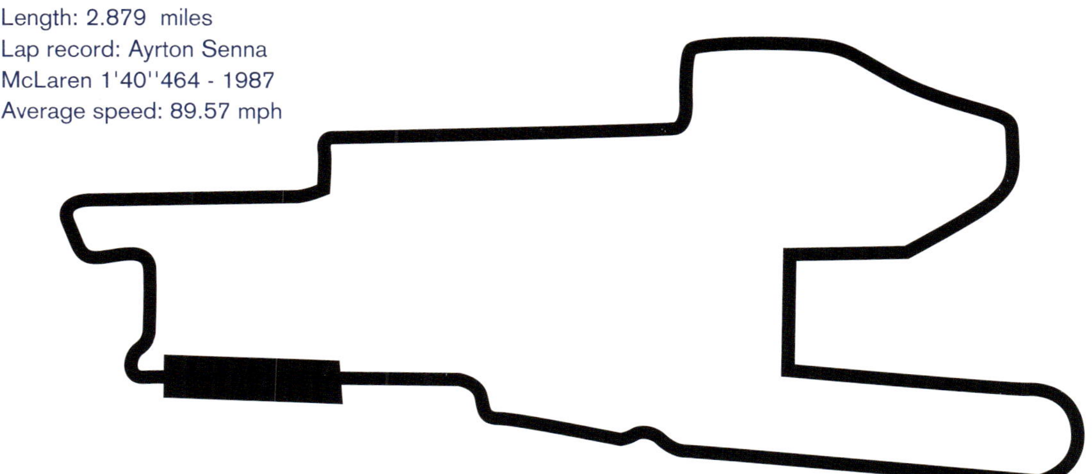

DALLAS

Street circuits have always presented unique challenges to F1 drivers, but the difficulties they faced at the first and last Dallas Grand Prix in 1984 exceeded everyone's expectations. For starters, the race was scheduled in the height of the Texas summer, with temperatures runnin above 100 degrees all weekend. As a consequence, th track's surface, which had not been tested prior to th event as normally required, simply melted away. In th race, half of the 26 starters crashed and only tw finished on the same lap as the Williams-Honda of Kek Rosberg, who kept his cool in the blistering heat an treacherous conditions to register his fourth Grand Pri win. Perhaps the race's defining moment was whe Nigel Mansell collapsed from exhaustion while attemptin to push his Lotus across the finish line. The scen perfectly epitomized the drama of a weekend in hell.

Length: 2.746 miles
Lap record: Niki Lauda
McLaren 1'45''353 - 1984
Average speed: 82.82 mph

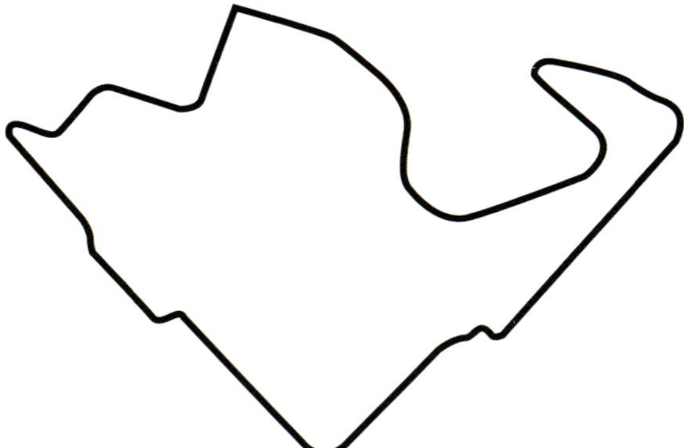

LEFT: Winner Keke Rosberg greeted by Sue Ellen Ewing/Linda Gray. BELOW LEFT: The Williams team exults as its driver takes the checkered flag.
BELOW: Extreme heat took its toll on drivers in 1984, including on Senna. RIGHT: Dallas' Grand Prix turned out to be a lot less thrilling than a roller coaster ride in 1984.

PHOENIX

After the demise of Detroit in 1988, Formula 1 supremo Bernie Ecclestone remained open to any initiative to keep a United States Grand Prix on the calendar. Phoenix promoted itself to the ranks of potential Grand Prix locations in a bid to gain exposure and encourage economic development in the area. The two parties came together in early 1989 and the desert city agreed to invest millions to run the U.S Grand Prix through its streets, hoping for a rich return. Phoenix did a remarkable job of putting the race together in just four months, and all was ready when Formula 1 came to town in June. Once again, drivers endured scorching heat, but unlike five years earlier, the track surface proved durable. Frenchman Alain Prost took top honors for McLaren in the inaugural event, while hometown boy Eddie Cheever - the only American on the grid - scored a sentimental victory when he brought his Arrows-Ford home in third place. The following year, young newcomer Jean Alesi almost created a major upset in his under-funded Tyrrell as he battled wheel-to-wheel with World Champion Ayrton Senna, finishing only a few seconds behind the great Brazilian. In 1991, despite his new McLaren-Honda not turning a wheel prior to arriving in Phoenix for the season-opening round, Senna took a comfortable win, beating the Ferrari of arch-rival Prost. Given the event's financial miseries, Phoenix organizer's had little choice but to throw in the towel at the end of their three-year term, thus leaving America without a Grand Prix for the first time since 1958.

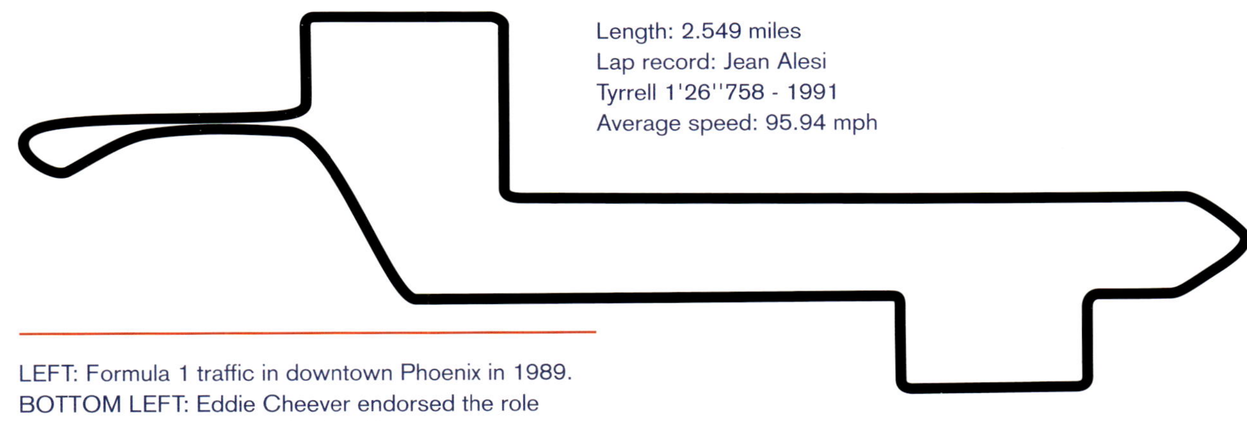

Length: 2.549 miles
Lap record: Jean Alesi
Tyrrell 1'26''758 - 1991
Average speed: 95.94 mph

LEFT: Formula 1 traffic in downtown Phoenix in 1989.
BOTTOM LEFT: Eddie Cheever endorsed the role of local hero when he finished 3rd in 1989.
BOTTOM: Tyrrell young gun Jean Alesi held his own against Ayrton Senna in 1990.

INDIANAPOLIS

After a nine year absence, Formula 1 found a new home in the United States at its most historic and monumental motor racing venue: the Indianapolis Motor Speedway. It took some time and concerted effort, but eventually Bernie Ecclestone convinced IMS President Tony George that Indy's status and mystique, associated with Grand Prix racing's prestige, constituted a recipe for success. A selective 13-turn infield road course running clockwise and linking parts of the famous oval was duly constructed, and in September 2000 the new United States Grand Prix exploded out of the gate as the best-attended Formula 1 race in the world with more than 250,000 spectators. The 2001 edition was overshadowed by the events of September 11. Still, a massive crowd packed the Brickyard to witness Mika Häkkinen's final victory of his Formula 1 career as he beat newly-crowned World Champion Michael Schumacher. The German ace was undeniably the king of F1's run at Indianapolis, winning five of his seven starts at the event. He enjoyed a less-than-satisfying victory in 2005 however, when only six cars competed in the race due to problems with tires supplied by Michelin. For safety reasons, drivers using the French manufacturer's rubber agreed to retire their car after the formation lap, leaving the six Bridgestone-shod machines to fight amongst themselves. Indy hosted the US Grand Prix on two more occasions, with Lewis Hamilton narrowly beating McLaren team mate Fernando Alonso in 2007, the event's final year. In the end, Tony George and Bernie Ecclestone mutually agreed to part ways, ultimately sealing the fate for Formula 1 in America. At least until 2012...

ABOVE: Kimi Räikkönen rides Indy's banking in 2001. LEFT: Schumacher, Massa and Fisichella on Victory Lane in 2006. RIGHT: The Brickyard hosted the United States Grand Prix from 2000 to 2007.

Length: 2.106 miles
Lap record: Rubens Barrichello
Ferrari 1'10''399 - 2004
Average speed: 133.201

UNITED STATES GRAND PRIX
INDIANAPOLIS
F1 Formula 1
HSBC
CHAMPAGNE MUMM

MONZANAPOLIS

RACE OF TWO WORLDS

In the late 1950s, the worlds of Grand Prix and Indy oval racing were pitted against each other at Monza in an amusing attempt to decide who the best drivers were. There was no real contest however.

They called it "Monzanapolis", or "The Race of Two Worlds". The event was intended as a contest between ten of the best drivers from Europe and an equal number from America, racing on Monza's oval circuit, with its high banking, in a counter-clockwise direction. The rules were those used at Indy, with 2.8 litre supercharged and 4.2 litre normally aspirated engine restrictions, while the format would include a distance of 500 miles divided into three separate 63-lap heats, the winner determined by the driver which finished all three heats with the highest average speed.

In June of 1957, USAC sent its volunteered teams and drivers to the inaugural running of "The Race of Two World". When the Americans arrived at Monza, they discovered that the European Formula 1 drivers would not compete, citing the risks associated with excessive speeds in a race they judged as "mass suicide"! Needless to say, the Indy drivers were unimpressed. Frenchman Jean Behra, driving a works Maserati, was one of two continental drivers who accepted the challenge, while the Scottish Ecurie Ecosse team, fresh from its win at Le Mans the week before, also sent three entries. Still, Jimmy Bryan emerged the overall victor, collecting a $26,801 check which was a hefty amount of money at that time. The following year, their egos blemished, the Europeans teams were out in full force to stop the Americans in their own back yard. Ferrari had three cars (with Phil Hill in one of them) while Maserati had a special Indy-type racer built for Stirling Moss called the Eldorado Special after its sponsor Eldorado ice cream. Fangio was driving with the Americans in the previous year's winner. There was no stopping Yank Jim Rathmann though in his Watson-Offy. Several European drivers actually fared well, but unaccustomed to the methanol fumes produced by the American engines, they were forced to stop, overwhelmed and intoxicated. It was the last edition of a series where in the end, Indy drivers proved once again that when it came to banked speedways, they were second to none.

LEFT: French driver Maurice Trintignant at full speed on Monza's banking at the wheel of the Kuzma-Offenhauser he shared with our very own A.J. Foyt in 1958. RIGHT: J.C. Agajanian's crew tends to Troy Ruttman's Kuzma-Offy.

YANKEES GO HOME!

Ten years after "The Race of Two Worlds", two Indycar drivers were back in action at Monza for what should have been their grand debut in Formula 1. Mario Andretti and Bobby Unser had both secured drives for the 1968 Italian Grand Prix, the first with Lotus and the second with the works BRM team.

The USAC rivals' season was still in full swing in the United States, with both men locked in a tight battle for the title, but for Monza they joined forces and travelled to Italy together in a mad-dash transatlantic double round trip stint. "Bobby and I were racing at the Hoosier 100 at Indy on the Saturday," Mario remembers, "so we were on an awfully tight schedule! I only got in about 20 minutes of track time in Friday's practice, but when I left, I was quickest at that stage." Mario Andretti's impressive lap times on his first official Formula 1 outing were also his last of the weekend. Both drivers did indeed race in the Hoosier 100 on Saturday but upon their tardy return to the Monza paddock on Sunday, they learned of their exclusion from the Grand Prix as officials invoked a sporting rule which prohibited a driver from taking part in two races in a 24-hour period! "That was all political stuff, that crap they pulled on us in Monza," Unser recounted in the book American Grand Prix. "They let us fly all that way for nothing. And then, we drove all the way to the airport like idiots, maniacs, tryin' to make it. I risked both Mario's and my life just getting to the race track. We ran on sidewalks through towns, Italian cops were wavin' their arms and yellin' at us, we just went and went. Mario'd read the signs, tell me where to go, and I'm drivin'. Stupidest thing I've ever done. And all the time, we wasn't gonna have a chance to run anyway!" Bobby Unser would get a chance to run in the US Grand Prix at Watkins Glen a few weeks later, albeit with a broken ankle contracted the day before in a basketball game. BRM supremo Louis Stanley urged the 1968 Indy 500 winner to drive so the team could collect some well negotiated starting money. "The doctor at the Glen gave me some pills to kill the pain," Unser remembers, "but they must have been mighty strong 'cause I wrecked the car, tore all four corners off it! It was just a piece of junk. They gave me the spare for the race which was made up for Rodriguez, but the transmission didn't work. That's when I also discovered that the engine I'd been using had 30 percent less power than Pedro's. Lou had promised me equal stuff, so I told him I'd been had and walked away. That was my last deal in Formula 1."

RIGHT: Andretti and Unser relax before Friday's practice at Monza, unaware of what the Italian officials had in store for the travelling duo. LEFT: Chapman oversees Andretti in what should have been Mario's F1 debut. BOTTOM: Unser's US Grand Prix efforts were thwarted after 19 laps by a faulty transmission.

GOODYEAR

CIRCUIT OF THE AMERICAS

BIRTH | VISION | ARCHITECT | FUTURE

Red Bull
TOTAL

BIRTH OF A CIRCUIT

by JULIE KOENIG LOIGNON
VICE PRESIDENT OF PUBLIC & COMMUNITY RELATIONS

In early 2010, if you had asked the average Austin resident about the fate of roughly 1,100 acres of undeveloped land just southeast of the city's international airport, it's doubtful anyone would have pegged the parcel as the perfect place for a purpose-built Grand Prix racecourse.

In a city that prides itself on its "weirdness," giving rise to the unexpected is routine. And in the early 2011, Circuit of The Americas™, the United States' most recent, and some say best, opportunity to create a lasting home for Formula 1™ racing was born. It wasn't an easy delivery. In fact, as labors go, this one was monumental. Construction, which started in January 2011, was often impacted by triple-digit heat, torrential rains and changes within the Circuit's ownership structure that briefly threatened to scuttle the project altogether. Its inaugural event, the 2012 FORMULA 1 UNITED STATES GRAND PRIX™ was subject to much political wrangling within the Formula 1 universe, as well as within state and local government circles, and was both on and off the official FIA Formula One World Championship calendar for a period of time. Fortunately, the Circuit's current owners saved the day in November 2011 by negotiating a new, 10-year deal with Formula 1 Supremo Bernie Ecclestone, thereby guaranteeing the return of F1™ racing to the United States for years to come.

Despite those early challenges, the dreams and determination of the dozens of investors that made the project possible overcame every obstacle, and by early 2012, most of the behind-the-scenes issues that complicated construction progress had been resolved. That paved the way for 1,700 Central Texas construction workers to fully focus on the task of building a world-class sports and entertainment venue in record time.

The innovative facility was designed by a noteworthy team of architects and engineers, including Austin-based Miro Rivera Architects, HKS Architects, STG Design and Tilke GmbH, the world-renowned German architectural-design firm that has created some of motorsports' modern masterpieces. Tilke-inspired racing circuits can be found in Abu Dhabi-United Arab Emirates, Austria, Bahrain, China, India, Indonesia, Ireland, Kazakhstan, Latvia, Malaysia, Romania, Russia, Singapore, South Korea, Spain and several circuits still under construction.

Circuit of The Americas consists of 375 acres of developed space, featuring a 3.4-mile, 20-turn racing circuit with challenging turns reminiscent of some of the great international racing circuits and stretches with significant elevation changes, including a 133-foot climb up to the track's signature Turn 1. Professional drivers who had the opportunity to test sections of the circuit while it was still under construction described it as being "amazing, challenging and something truly unique" in the world of motorsports.

Circuit of The Americas is so impressive that American motorsports legend and former Formula 1 Champion driver Mario Andretti eagerly signed on as its official public "ambassador" six months before the grand opening. The always energetic Andretti was like a kid in a candy store during his first visit to the racetrack on June 7, 2012, where he spent the day "tweeting" images from the course's iconic angles before burning a little rubber behind the wheel of Circuit founding partner Bobby Epstein's sports-utility vehicle.

"Formula 1's return to the United States is so exciting for racing fans, especially at a purpose-built facility," Andretti said following his test drive. "The project has a strong team

ABOVE: Circuit President Steve Sexton addresses the crowd at the COTA construction ceremony (April 21, 2012) LEFT: David Coulthard's Red Bull carves the path for COTA as he powers through a turn during the construction stage (August 21, 2011) NEXT PAGE: Turn 7 and Turn 8 under another beautiful Texas sun (August 2012)

behind it. The track design has really come together, and it's clear that this will be a phenomenal venue for a variety of premium motorsports."

Circuit of The Americas features a main grandstand with seating for 9,000 spectators, including permanent suites and semi-private, loge-level seating. The massive, 270,000-square foot Paddock Building features 34 individual garages and two upper levels of premium hospitality space. The 40,000-square foot media and conference center will be home to everything from working journalists to business seminars, auto shows and other large-scale events, while the 5,500-square foot, on-site medical facility offers state-of-the-art paramedic care for competitors and spectators alike.

One of the circuit's most remarkable features is the amphitheater situated at the base of the venue's main entrance, called the Grand Plaza. The Tower Amphitheater, so named for the 251-foot observation tower that stretches high above it, is an expansive entertainment space accommodating 15,000 guests. In July 2012, Circuit of The Americas announced an agreement with Live Nation, the world's largest live music and entertainment company, to bring national touring acts to the Circuit beginning in 2013. The Tower Amphitheater, now the largest theater of its kind in Central Texas, will feature some of the country's most popular performers on a year-round basis and add to Austin's legacy as the "Live Music Capital of the World."

As origin stories go, Circuit of The Americas' is one for the record books, and woven into its tale are the personal histories of thousands of people—from owners to employees to fans—who shared in the experience of bringing America's newest center for sports, entertainment and business to life. There are plenty of pages left to write in this very special story, and the entire Circuit of The Americas family looks forward to what the next chapter brings.

TOP: Our COTA Ambassador, Mario Andretti drives around the course (June 7, 2012)
ABOVE: Ex-F1 driver Bob Bondurant takes his Corvette through the paces at the circuit during the late stages of construction (August 8, 2012)
RIGHT: An aerial view of the circuit's brilliant design and challenging lay-out (August 2012)

TWO MEN, ONE VISION

BOBBY & RED

The return of Formula 1 to the United States represents, in itself, an important milestone for all those involved in the sport, and for Texas. Designing and erecting the first purpose-built Grand Prix facility in the country, one which doubles as a world-class destination for performance, education and business, was a monumental task. It took careful planning and execution, with all the right people focused on the job at hand. But above all, it required a vision, the essence of which was supplied by Bobby Epstein and Red McCombs.

A lifetime Texan and a Plan II honors program graduate of the University of Texas at Austin, Bobby Epstein spent most of his professional career managing or trading fixed-income securities. In the early 90s, Epstein founded his first business, a broker dealer specializing in mortgage-backed bonds. Upon selling that company in 1995, Epstein started Prophet Capital Management, a business that has afforded him the opportunity to enter into several business ventures and to be a founding partner in Circuit of The Americas. "After 25 years of sitting at a desk and looking at a screen, I decided the opportunity to build something with such massive local impact was too good to pass up," Epstein said. "It's nice to create something unique and in a way that has never been done before. We're trying to rewrite the book on how to marry racing and entertainment."

In 2005, at the height of the real estate bubble, Mr. Epstein bought his first significant piece of development property. Located southeast of Austin, the land was originally purchased with the idea that the growing housing market would soon overtake this overlooked, and somewhat neglected, part of the Travis County. When the housing bubble burst, Epstein frequently mentioned to friends that he wanted to put into the property an amusement, entertainment and sports venue, modeled somewhat after the success of sports complexes in the Arlington, Texas, area, which is home to the National Football League's Dallas Cowboys and Major League Baseball's Texas Rangers. He felt strongly that the growing number of communities throughout Central Texas could support more family-friendly activities and that visitors would find the additions a wonderful compliment to the expanding number of reasons to visit the area. Now, he just needed to find a few others that felt the same way. "When one thinks of success, autos, sports, giving and Texas, all roads lead to Red McCombs," Epstein said. "When we were thinking of who would make a great partner, Red was a natural, first choice. Without Red and his top lieutenant Rad Weaver, I'm not sure that I would have made it to opening day.

Billy Joe "Red" McCombs welcomed the change to be part of the team of investors bringing Formula 1 to the Lone Star State. McCombs joined the Circuit of The Americas team in July 2010 and through this new venture he is extending his legacy as a Texas businessman with an

COTA's main straight basks in serenity while it awaits the frenzy and rage of race day.

entrepreneurial spirit and great love of sports and automobiles. McCombs' entrepreneurial beginnings were in the tiny town of Spur, Texas, where he sold bags of peanuts as a young boy. In 1958, he moved to San Antonio in 1958, and eventually started selling used cars in Corpus Christie at the tender age of 20. From those humble beginnings grew the McCombs Automotive, which allowed McCombs to branch out into other business ventures and enjoy success in almost every endeavor he's tried. In 1972, McCombs co-founded Clear Channel Communications with Lowry Mays, which grew into a world leader in radio and outdoor advertising. Through his other ventures -including McCombs Energy, Koontz McCombs real estate, McCombs Ranches and McCombs Partners -McCombs continues to indulge his entrepreneurial spirit. Aside from his passion for business, McCombs is an avid sports aficionado. He is the former owner of the San Antonio Spurs, Denver Nuggets, and Minnesota Vikings. As an example of his devotion to the University of Texas Longhorns, where he once attended class, McCombs can always be spotted wearing a ring given to him by the school's football team. His likeness can be seen at Darrell Royal Memorial Football Stadium, where a statue of McCombs stands in an area now known as the "Red Zone." McCombs is also an inductee of the National Football Foundation's College Football Hall of Fame and the Texas Sports Hall of Fame. It's that love of sports, combined with his success in the automotive world that made an investment in Circuit of The Americas such an appealing idea.

"Bringing Formula 1 to Austin is a tremendous opportunity for the city and State of Texas, given F1's global appeal and significant economic impact," McCombs noted. "For me, investing in Circuit of The Americas is a good business venture and chance to be part of something special. I never thought I'd be taking on a project like this one in my mid-80s, but it's been lots of fun and will mean great things for Central Texas."

As chairman and founding partner of the Circuit, Bobby Epstein has personally overseen almost every aspect of the venue's creation and execution, from investor recruitment and long-range business planning to individual building design elements and racetrack safety features. He has shepherded the young company through accelerated construction schedules and public relations challenges, along with all of the normal challenges that come with starting a private business with private equity…and blood, sweat and tears. The vision, passion and persistence shared by Bobby Epstein and Red McCombs have helped define the Circuit of The Americas brand and set the stage for remarkable things to happen as the facility and its business matures. Most important, their determination to offer their fellow Texans, and guests from around the world, a premier sports and entertainment experience is part of what makes Circuit of The Americas a world-class destination.

ABOVE: Bobby Epstein, Mario Andretti and executive Bruce Knox survey construction from the top of Turn 1 (June 7, 2012)
RIGHT: Tilke architectural rendering of the circuit that came to reality with the inaugural USGP November 16-18, 2012.

CHIEF ARCHITECT

HERMANN TILKE

Renowned German architect Hermann Tilke has been at the forefront of circuit conception for almost two decades, erecting state-of-the-art race tracks all over the world. An impassioned motor sport fan, who once raced touring cars in Europe, the 56-year-old civil engineer readily admits combining pleasure with business when it comes to circuit design.

Located in Aachen, western Germany, his company, Tilke Engineering & Architects, relies on a large interdisciplinary skilled team of more than 350 engineers and architects devoted to numerous tailor-made projects in the racing, sports and leisure, hotel and industrial arenas. As a world leading designer for racetracks, Tilke and his team have conceived eleven venues in Formula 1's current portfolio of races. But when speaking about his involvement with the Circuit of Americas, which also showcases the expertise and work of many Texan companies, he has nothing but high praise for the facility's natural environment and the impressive design it inspired.

"The area's natural topography and a lack of effective constraints enabled us to conceive a very selective layout", Tilke explains, "with several elevation changes and a series of fast flowing sections, tight hairpins and a long straight. All in all, COTA boasts all the qualities of a natural road course, not unlike the Istanbul Otodrom which we designed in Turkey."

A change of scenery obviously leads to a different design approach, so how does COTA compare to Tilke's previous realizations conducted in China, the United Arab Emirates and in Europe ?

"We're actually used to working in different contexts and understanding them," the German confirms. "For us, it's an asset we incorporate into a design which must embody a country's culture and background. To achieve this, we also cooperate extensively with local contractors and suppliers. In the United States, the emphasis is put on the machines rather than the human resource when one builds a racetrack. At one stage, we had 1,200 workers on the COTA site while 10,000 were required to build the Abu Dhabi facility. Proce-

Former racer Hermann Tilke has been Formula 1's Chief Architect for over ten years, combining his skills in architecture and civil engineering to provide complete solutions for motor racing.

dures may vary, but generally design briefs remains the same. From the first initial concept to detailed design, construction supervision and project management, we handle everything and that's really what sets us apart. Promoters who work with us know they will save time thanks to our experience and ability in resolving difficulties, simply because we encountered them before."

Regardless of a venue's environment and the characteristics of its layout, Tilke insists there is no magic recipe in creating a facility which will guarantee exciting racing.

"A lot depends on the site itself, and in COTA's case we were offered good land, acreage and relief. We always try to create areas and sequences which enhance overtaking, with a more technical section often followed by a fast portion. To this effect, we also do a lot of simulator work with former F1 driver Alex Wurz in order to evaluate driving difficulties and attempt to render things more selective. But the level is such in Formula 1 that technically, we're close to perfection. You need drivers to approach the limit in order to generate an exciting race and overtaking. It's also essential to take into account spectator vantage points and design areas where things happen in view of the grandstands. It's all about creating a great atmosphere for the fans, with a thrilling stadium-like feel."

Once work on a facility begins and the heavy machinery is put into motion, a major challenge, and priority, is obviously remaining on schedule. Despite a specific period when all parties involved were under a fair amount of pressure, Hermann Tilke always remained confident in achieving COTA's deadline.

"At one stage, we lost three months, but it all worked out in the end. There are always inevitable delays when you're starting from scratch, and short deadlines are part of the job description. In hindsight, we faced a much tougher time in New Delhi when designing the track for the Indian Grand Prix. COTA provided its fair share of challenges, but everyone pulled out all the stops to deliver an outstanding racing facility, without sacrificing any aspect, and least of all security, to time."

Going back to the importance of integrating elements of local culture in a racetrack design, Formula 1's chief architect embedded COTA with a few concepts and ideas directly inspired by the city of Austin's urbanity.

"The circuit's main entry features a 22-story steel structure with an observation deck that will overlook the track, while an amphitheater destined to host major concerts is located at the basis of the tower. These were designed by Miro Rivera Architects from Austin. COTA isn't just a world-class motor racing facility, it's also a modern and multi functional complex offering a whole array of business and entertainment activities. Austin is a young and vibrant city, and we believe the Circuit of Americas properly reflects these modern virtues."

RIGHT: A view from the exit of Turn 20, from where the cars accelerate on to the main straight and climb to the first corner - the highest point of the circuit.

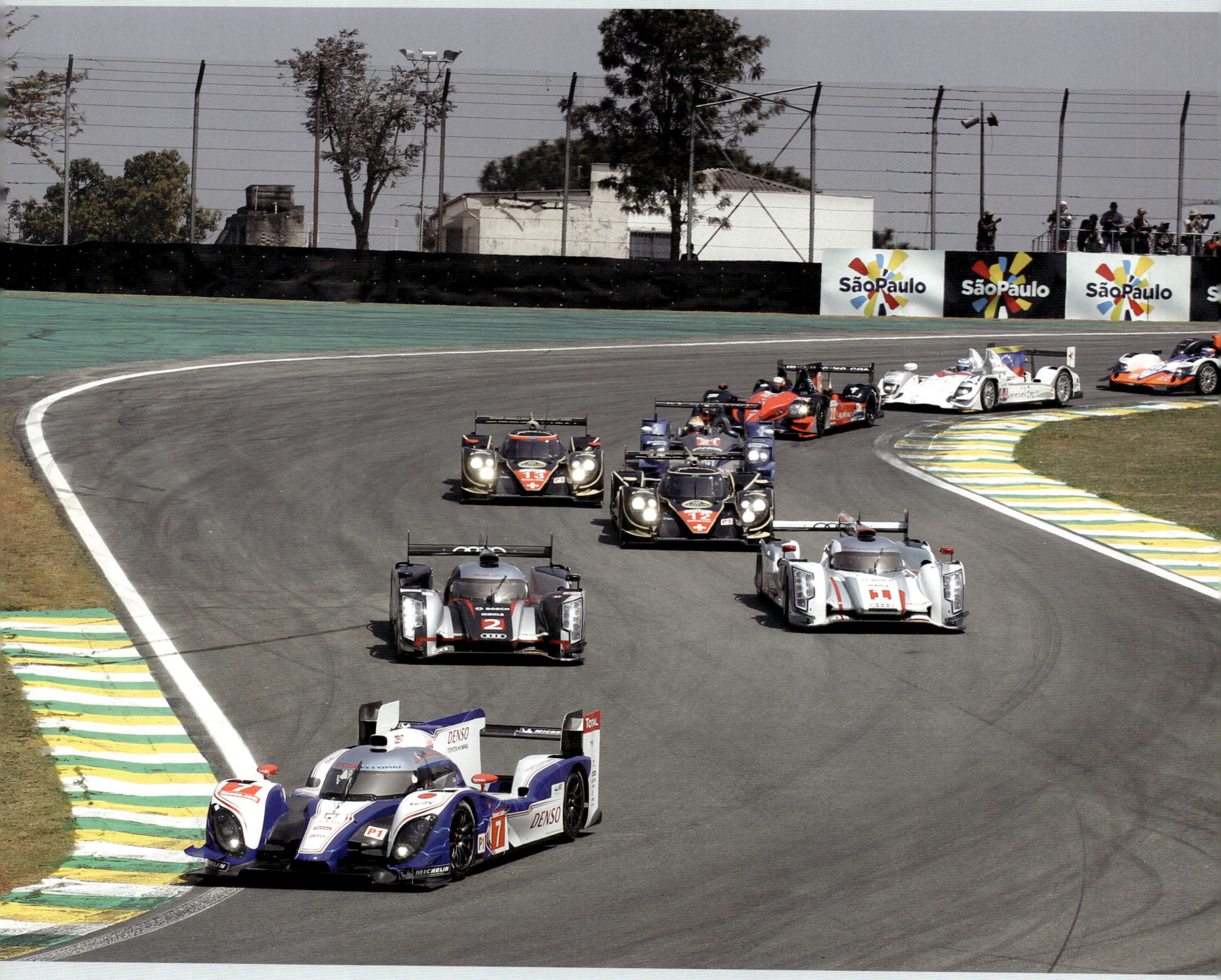

THE NEXT CHAPTER

by JULIE KOENIG LOIGNON

So, after you build, staff and program a brand new sports and entertainment venue — and play host to a sellout crowd at one of the world's premier sporting events — all in less than two years' time, what's next?

The ambitious team at Circuit of The Americas will celebrate the successful completion of its first FORMULA 1 UNITED STATES GRAND PRIX™ by preparing to host four new racing series at its Austin, Texas, home, including V8 Supercars, American Le Mans, the FIA World Endurance Championship and MotoGP.

In addition, The Tower Amphitheater, opening in the spring of 2013, will host a full schedule of live performances as Central Texas' newest home for premium entertainment. With live music and entertainment powerhouse Live Nation recruiting the talent, "The Tower" is sure to make some noise on the national music scene.

Future development plans include an on-track driving experiences, a go-kart and off-road track, other sporting events, music festivals, facility tours, conventions and seminars, hospitality rentals, educational partnerships and a variety of sustainability initiatives to help Circuit of The Americas continue to give back to the community it calls "home."

Being a good neighbor and minimizing its impact on the environment is also a top priority for the circuit. In fact, Circuit of The Americas is the first purpose-built Formula 1™ racing facility to become a member of the Green Sports Alliance, a non-profit organization made up of more than 40 professional and collegiate sports teams and nearly 90 sports venues with a mission to help enhance their environmental performance.

After an action-packed launch, there's much to look forward to at America's newest center for sports, business and leisure as Circuit of The Americas revs its engine and expands its offerings in Central Texas and beyond.

As America's premier racing facility, COTA will play host to various motor sport events ranging from MotoGP to the World Endurance Championship, while the center will also feature prominent music events.

GIVES YOU
NGS
19
MAGNETI
MARELLI
Red Bull
Red Bull

STATISTICS

FACTS & STATS

Two American World Champions
-Phil Hill (1961/Ferrari)
-Mario Andretti (1978/Lotus)

The country with the greatest number of World Champions(14) is Great Britain. **The United States is 10th.**

Five American drivers have won at least 1 Grand Prix
- Mario Andretti = 12 wins (SA 71/Ferrari, JAP 76-USA 77-SPA 77-FRA 77-ITA 77-ARG 78-BEL 78-SPA 78-FRA 78-GER 78-PB 78/Lotus)
- Dan Gurney = 4 wins (FRA 62/Porsche, FRA 64-MEX 64/Brabham, BEL 67/Eagle)
- Phil Hill = 3 wins (ITA 60-HOL 61-ITA 61/Ferrari)
- Peter Revson = 2 wins (GB 73-CAN 73/McLaren)
- Richie Ginther = 1 win (MEX 65/Honda)

With 223 victories, Great Britain holds the record for the greatest number of wins per country. **The United States is 11th with 22 wins** (Indy 500 winners are not included).

Four Americans accomplished at least one pole position in qualifying
- Mario Andretti = 18 poles from 1968 to 1982 with Ferrari and Lotus
- Phil Hill = 6 poles in 1960 and 1961 with Ferrari
-Dan Gurney = 3 poles from 1962 to 1964 with Porsche and Brabham
- Peter Revson = 1 pole in 1972 with McLaren

With 28 pole positions, the **United States is 11th in country standings**. Great Britain leads with 210 pole positions.

Excluding those who ran in the Indy 500 when it counted for the Formula 1 World Championship, 47 American drivers have started 443 Grands Prix since 1950.
Harry Schell was the first, (Monaco 1950/Cooper), and Scott Speed was the last (Europe 2007/Toro Rosso):

Driver	Starts
- Eddie Cheever	132
- Mario Andretti	128
- Dan Gurney	86
- Harry Schell	56
- Richie Ginther	52
- Phil Hill	49
- Masten Gregory	38
- Brett Lunger	32
- Peter Revson	30
- Scott Speed	28
- Danny Sullivan	15
- Mark Donohue	14
- Michael Andretti	13
- Ronnie Bucknum, Jim Hall and Georges Follmer	11
- Bob Bondurant	9
- Carroll Shelby	8
- Pete Lovely	7
- Tony Settember and Hap Sharp	6
- Skip Barber and Sam Tingle	5
- Danny Ongais	4
- Chuck Daigh and Fred Wacker	3
- Roger Penske, Roger Ward, Sam Posey, Bobby Rahal, Walt Hangsen and John Fitch	2
- Harry Blanchard, Jay Chamberlain, George Constantine, Mike Fisher, Fred Gamble, Gus Hutchison, Tim Mayer, Herbert Mackey-Fraser, Robert O'Brien, Bobby Unser, Lance Reventlow, Lloyd Ruby, Troy Ruttman, Pete Ryan and Bob Said	1

Four Americans hold at least one lap record
- Mario Andretti = 10 lap records from 1971 to 1978 with Ferrari, Parnelli and Lotus
- Phil Hill = 6 lap records from 1958 to 1961 with Ferrari
- Dan Gurney = 6 lap records from 1963 to 1967 with Brabham and Eagle
- Richie Ginther = 3 lap records from 1961 to 1966 with Ferrari and Honda

With 25 lap records, **the United States is 10th in country standings.** Great Britain leads with 199 lap records.

To this day, American drivers have been on 93 Formula 1 podiums.
Masten Gregory was the first (Monaco 1957/Maserati/3rd), and Michael Andretti was the last (Italy 1993/McLaren/3rd).

Excluding the Indy 500, six American teams have started at least one Grand Prix since 1950.
Three teams have won a Formula 1 Grand Prix.
- Shadow (1 win = Austria 77/Alan Jones, 3 poles, 2 lap records 7 podiums, 104 GP, 67,5 pts, 50 laps in the lead)
- Penske (1 win = Austria 76/John Watson, 3 podiums, 23 pts, 40 GP, 45 laps in the lead)
- Eagle (1 win = Belgium 67/Dan Gurney, 2 lap records, 3 podiums, 17 pts, 25 GP, 19 laps in the lead)

LEFT: Scott Speed's Toro Rosso lifts a wheel at Monaco in 2007

F1 2012
Formula 1
F1 2012
Formula 1
F1 2012
Formula 1
F1 2012
Formula 1

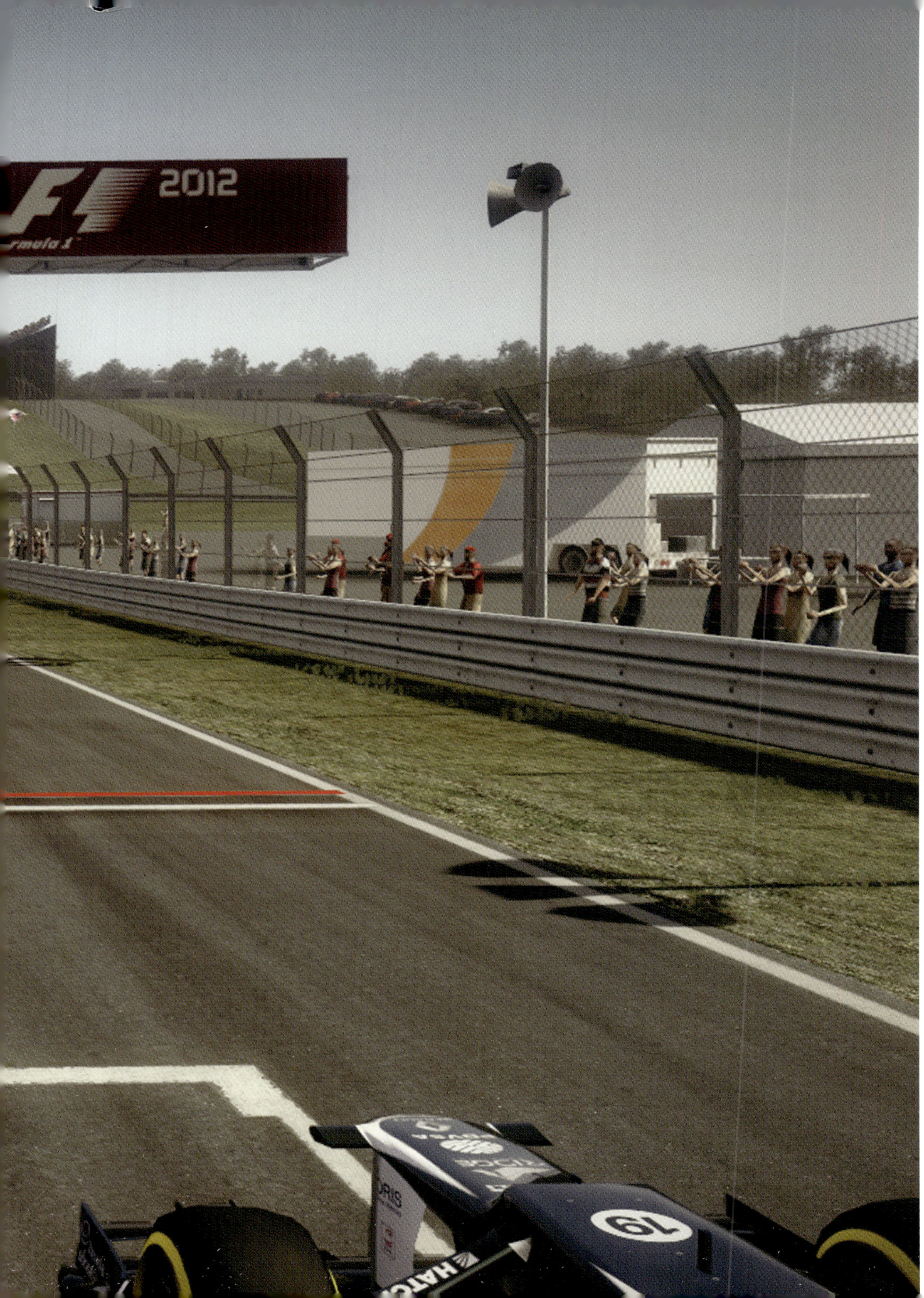

Good luck to all at the Circuit of The Americas! Being the home of official FORMULA ONE™ video games, Codemasters is honored to be associated with the sport's return to America.

This year has been very special for us, as we had the honor of exclusively unveiling the Circuit of The Americas track in this year's F1 2012™ video game. Visit www.formula1-game.com for information.

We've also recently launched F1 Online: The Game™, a free-to-play video game that can be played in a browser www.f1onlinethegame.com Soon we'll release a brand new "family friendly" FORMULA ONE video game in F1 RACE STARS™, which sees all the drivers recreated as cartoon heroes and racing on fantastical tracks. Visit www.F1RaceStars.com for more.

With all of our FORMULA ONE video games, our hope is to introduce the sport's culture to younger generations. We are especially eager to see new FORMULA ONE champions emerging from America, where motorsport is king.

All the team at Codemasters

PAUL HENRI & BERNARD CAHIER

Frenchman Bernard Cahier was motor racing's first true photo-journalist. He was only 17 when he enrolled into the resistance during the Second World War, later joining General Philippe Leclerc's 2nd Armored Division. A few years after the war he headed to the United States to study at UCLA where he met his future wife Joan. When he took a job at Roger Barlow's foreign car dealership in Los Angeles, Bernard became acquainted with fellow salesman Phil Hill and mechanic Richie Ginther who would both later achieve international fame in F1. Cahier also cut his teeth competing in an MG before returning to Europe in 1952 to embark on his distinguished career as a photographer and journalist, becoming an eminent figure in Grand Prix paddocks for over thirty years. Through his American connections, he acted as a public relations consultant for Goodyear and was also instrumental in helping moviemaker John Frankenheimer produce the epic film "Grand Prix". Bernard Cahier also founded and was the President of the International Racing Press Association. His son Paul-Henri followed in his footsteps when he became a notable photographer in his own right. He has followed Formula 1 for thirty years and his outstanding work is published in countries all over the world.

PHILLIP van OSTEN

Motor racing was a backdrop from the outset in Phillip van Osten's life. Born in Southern California in 1958, he grew up with the sights and sounds of fast cars thanks to his father, Dick van Osten, an editor and writer for Auto Speed and Sport and Motor Trend. Phillip's passion for racing grew even more when his family moved to Europe and he became acquainted with the extraordinary world of Grand Prix racing. He was an early contributor to the monthly French F1i Magazine, often providing a historic or business perspective on Formula 1's affairs. In 2012, he co-authored along with fellow journalist Pierre Van Vliet the English-language adaptation of a limited edition book devoted to the great Belgian driver Jacky Ickx. Phillip is also a commentator for Belgian broadcaster Be.TV for the US Indycar series.